Emily Scott

Time & Tide

Emily Scott

Recipes and stories from my coastal kitchen

Time & Tide

Photography by Kristin Perers

Hardie Grant
BOOKS

With love, and may the table always come first.

THE SHIPPING FORECAST ISSUED BY THE MET OFFICE, ON BEHALF OF THE MARITIME AND COASTGUARD AGENCY:

GENERAL SYNOPSIS AT 0600
LOW FITZROY 999 SLOW-MOVING, FILLING 1011 BY 0600 TOMORROW.

LUNDY, FASTNET
NORTHEAST BACKING NORTH OR NORTHWEST, 3 TO 5. SLIGHT OR MODERATE. FAIR. GOOD.

THE SHIPPING FORECAST IS BROADCAST ON LONGWAVE BBC RADIO 4 AT FOUR PRECISE TIMES A DAY: 0048, 0520, 1201 AND 1754. USING A UNIQUE AND DETAILED SCALE SYSTEM, IT TELLS SAILORS AND FISHERMEN ON BRITAIN'S AND IRELAND'S COASTAL WATERS WHAT WEATHER TO EXPECT IN THE COMING HOURS. THE FORECAST WAS FIRST DEVELOPED BY THE WORLD'S FIRST WEATHERMAN, VICE-ADMIRAL ROBERT FITZROY, IN FEBRUARY 1861. THE AREA OF LUNDY IS THE NAME FOR CORNWALL'S LOCAL WATERS.

Introduction: A Call to the Coast

This is my life by the sea, where hawthorn and gorse bloom and tamarisk trees meet the edges of the cliffs, where wild coastal flowers – fennel, teasels and ox daisies – drift down to the edge of the sea. Grassy hillsides are laden with bracken. Gateways lead the way around the rocky landscape of North Cornwall, the place I call home. Colourful flowers and herbs line the wooden fences and stony pathways that run along the rugged, carved headlands, wild and beautiful through each season. Sea mists, chase the blues of the swirling skies. The granite colour of the roaring sea, merging sometimes into all the hues of blue and green. The sound of the screeching gulls and the echoes of the other sea birds swooping along the cliff side, all busy with their day. Quintessential slate-hung cottages look out to sea. Babbling streams. Dragonflies and butterflies. Rock pooling shoreside, a world of wonder – so many textures and colours, and the sea life – botanicals, crabs, shrimps, limpets, anemones, starfish, whelks and more. Leaning over the small pools on the rocky shoreline, both as a child and later with my own children, has always been a seaside highlight for me. Cornwall is beautiful, whatever the season, and will always lift your spirits.

I am so excited that you are returning to the seaside in beautiful Cornwall with me, to discover my coastal kitchen, which is very much at the heart of everything I do. In my first book, *Sea & Shore*, I took you through the seasons by the sea with chapters on Spring Tides, Summer Seas, High Summer, Autumn Tides, Noël and Winter Seas. In *Time & Tide*, I will take you through the heart of my kitchen as the days unfold in moments of time, to tell you about what is important to me and brings me joy. From my style and how to keep things simple yet thoughtful, to my favourite times of the day and the importance of making time. I begin with Rise & Shine, and the recipes with which I love to start my day; then move on to Morning Café, a ritual that will never be broken; on to My Kitchen Table and the recipes that have been important to me and my family; never far from the water, I share some of my favourite recipes for on the go in On the Boat; slowing down for relaxed Seaside Soirées and Lazy Sunday Lunches. Last, but not least, in Time to Preserve I share my love for preserving ingredients so they can be enjoyed throughout the year.

Join me to discover recipes from my coastal garden, for long lunches, beach days, boat days, salty swims and sunsets by the sea, all using beautiful ingredients, with nostalgia and provenance always at the core of my cooking.

Seaside Madeleines

Before we continue, let's stop and enjoy a quiet moment. I have baked you some seaside madeleines.

I have tried to perfect these beautiful light sponges, for which I have had great affection over the years. Hot from the oven and brushed with warm apricot jam, one is never enough. I use recycled scallop shells as madeleine moulds and they work beautifully.

MAKES ABOUT 12

- 100 g (3½ oz) unsalted butter, plus extra for greasing
- 100 g (3½ oz/generous ¾ cup) plain (all-purpose) flour, plus extra for dusting
- ¼ teaspoon baking powder
- pinch of Cornish sea salt
- 2 large free-range eggs
- zest of 1 lemon
- 100 g (3½ oz/scant ½ cup) golden caster (superfine) sugar
- 3 tablespoons apricot jam, warmed, for brushing
- icing (confectioner's) sugar, for dusting

Gently melt the butter in a pan, then allow to cool.

In a mixing bowl, sift together the flour and baking powder, then add the salt.

Combine the eggs, lemon zest and sugar in a stand mixer and beat on a medium spped until the mixture has thickened.

Fold the dry ingredients into the egg mixture, then pour in the melted cooled butter and stir together. Cover and chill the batter in the refrigerator for at least 1 hour (see note).

Preheat the oven to 200°C (180°C fan/400°F/Gas 6). If using scallop shells as your moulds, wash and scrub them, then dry, brush with butter and dust with flour, tapping out any excess flour. If using regular madeleine moulds, simply butter and dust in the same way.

Ladle the batter into the buttered and floured moulds and bake for 8–10 minutes.

Remove from the oven and transfer to a wire rack to cool slightly. Eat warm, brushed with warm apricot jam and dusted with icing sugar. I love madeleines this way, but of course dipping the ends in melted chocolate is also extraordinarily good.

COOK'S NOTE If you have time, it's best if you can leave the batter to rest for at least 1 hour or – if you can get ahead – overnight. These are best eaten immediately and if there happens to be any left over, they make great sponges for tiramisu or trifle. Wonderful with morning coffee or delicious dipped in a sweet Sauternes after supper.

Time & Tide

(BEYOND THE SHORE)

There is magic in colour. Time and colour are interconnected. From the summer solstice when the sun is high, marked on the longest day in June, to the shortest day in December when daylight is limited, whatever the season, or time of day, there is colour. And where there is colour we see the passage of time. I also see emotions in terms of colours and they move like the energy of the tide, washing in and out, never late, simply on time in their own time. It is easy sometimes to take this for granted, but whatever the season, day or time, I will always find beauty in the different colours and scents that surround me.

Oceans cover much of the planet, from the turquoise, warm waters of the Indian and Pacific Oceans to the cold north Arctic Ocean and the vast Atlantic, the latter of which I feel I know reasonably well as I spend much of my time in it, on it or by it. I often look out to sea and am in awe of the sheer amount of water we are surrounded by, how beautiful it is and how important it feels to me. Driven by the moon and the sun, the power of the tides has huge significance in my life.

Every day, twice a day, without fail, the tide comes in and goes out again. A ritual each day is to check the tides. Without thinking, it just happens – a part of living and working by the sea. The long waves that move across the water are fascinating and beautiful – a natural wonder of our world. I love the wonders of the sea throughout each season and time of day, from the stormy colder tides of winter to the glassy blues of high summer days. It is said that time and tide wait for no man – a saying that always makes me grasp the moment. Don't delay.

Time feels like it goes on forever – sometimes I get lost in time and other times it feels like a drag. Writing these words, I am in the moment, and then suddenly it is gone from me as I try to grasp and hold on to every minute. Counting down days, wishing time away – we all do this. Often, I find myself looking ahead, when really I should be still, learning to be more peaceful and at ease with the passing of time. Lean into time rather than letting time pass you by. The one lesson I have learned is that the more relaxed you are mentally and physically, the more you enjoy life and the faster time passes.

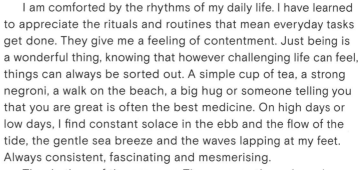

I am comforted by the rhythms of my daily life. I have learned to appreciate the rituals and routines that mean everyday tasks get done. They give me a feeling of contentment. Just being is a wonderful thing, knowing that however challenging life can feel, things can always be sorted out. A simple cup of tea, a strong negroni, a walk on the beach, a big hug or someone telling you that you are great is often the best medicine. On high days or low days, I find constant solace in the ebb and the flow of the tide, the gentle sea breeze and the waves lapping at my feet. Always consistent, fascinating and mesmerising.

The rhythms of the seasons. Time passes through each season slowly. I love waking up to my favourite autumnal days; the trees appearing bare as their leaves fall to the ground creating a carpet of burnt orange, browns and yellows. Colour on a grey day. Wood smoke fills the air, wafting over the slate-hung rooftops each day until winter says hello, with Christmas to fill our hearts and all that cheer. All wrapped up as colder than it looks. And just as we are becoming weary of the dark, short days, spring arrives with bulbs of colour and the chorus of birds all with something to say. Then the golden days of summer with flowers and smiles all round.

Days by the sea. Starry skies, frost at midnight, sunrise, tide on the turn, soft winter light, bright shining summer light, soft sea breezes, biting winter winds – all are different but equally beautiful. This sense of place moves me like the tide, out and back in again, chasing all moods, weathers, moments of life and time. Cornwall: 8 a.m., noon, 5 p.m. ... Golden sunlight, sunkissed, windswept. Happy anytime.

Rituals & Routines

(A SENSE OF BALANCE)

I love to hate routine – the tick of the clock, from weekdays to the always much-needed weekend, the change of seasons, a new day. From the sound of my alarm waking me in the darker mornings of winter to being woken by the seagulls crying in the skies like impatient children in the lighter months, there is something overwhelmingly comforting about routine, structure, order, control, and – again – a sense of place. The routine of pulling my favourite jumper over my pyjamas, turning on the same lamps and opening the shutters to see a glimpse of the day, I make my way downstairs in the beautiful quietness of the house as it slowly wakes. Inca wags her tail from her basket as I whisper good morning. Kettle on. That first cup of tea of the day is always the best one, in my view.

Morning routine. One thing at a time. A quick look at my emails, the news and always Instagram, planning my next square to share or looking at other people's adventures and everydays. Depending on the day ahead, I organise myself and my thoughts. I give myself some time: decide on something to wear that makes me feel good and always do my make-up. Rushing and not bothering always leaves me in a bad mood and I then feel off balance for the rest of the day. Breakfast on a college day for Evie, my daughter (my boys now away from home). I still always lay the table as I did when my children were growing up and light candles. The comforting noise of Radio 4 in the background. I try to take time to catch up with Evie before her day. These moments I find so precious. Dippy egg or maybe scrambled, toast and Marmite or porridge on colder days; on warmer days, summer fruits and yoghurt. The bus run. We are always running slightly behind, but we have never missed the bus (our claim to fame).

Checking on the tides, I head to Crantock beach, a place with which I have become more familiar since moving further west. I am getting to know the cliff edges and the ever-changing shapes of the sea, the broad sand dunes between the headlands of Pentire East and Pentire Point West. The dunes rise steeply and undulate along the coastline as far as the eye can see, home to jackdaws, fulmars, gulls and pigeons, who can be seen nesting next to the coast path. A sanctuary of beauty, there is no better way to start my day. At low tide, I walk across the beach breathing in the new day. If the tide is high, I walk along the narrow cliff path, watching Inca run energetically through the grasses, wishing I was as fit as her (but knowing that is the most ridiculous thought).

Home briefly, I next head out along the coastal road to my restaurant by the sea in Watergate Bay, a place that has become a home from home. Built on the sea wall, it looks out towards the miles and miles of Atlantic Ocean. A dream opportunity by the sea. I am always early, discussing, checking menus, arranging tables, organising plants and herbs, dressing the set and catching up with my team. As my team has grown, my routine has slightly changed. Gone are the days of me doing every service and working – apron on – every hour. There is now more balance and more time for the other opportunities that have come my way. Where is Emily? I am never far away.

Lunch and supper service, my restaurant runs Tuesday through to Saturday. I am always pushing harder, trying to do better. When you work for yourself there is never an end to your day. I often find I wake in the early hours and lie awake thinking of words to write, so I am often found at my desk writing in the early morning, not wanting to miss a word or a thought. I genuinely have a passion for what I do. There are always challenges, but I'm so happy to have found my place.

Time & Place

(SHADES OF MY WORLD)

I write and speak a lot about a sense of place and taking time. For me, that is so important in every aspect of my life, in the kitchen, at home and at my restaurant, as in everything I do. Being considered and thoughtful, taking time to think before you speak or to enjoy moments instead of rushing from one thing to another. In my view, food is best when eaten seasonally and gathered with excitement and enthusiasm. By that, I mean thinking about the time of year, what is in season and how to cook and care for the wonderful things that are brought to us. We all know that feeling of the holiday blues, of returning home after creating wonderful memories and recreating dishes that don't taste quite the same as they did where you were in that moment. Cooking within the seasons and having a strong sense of place is what I firmly believe in, as well as making time to come together whatever the time of day, month or year.

In these chapters, I create recipes that I think narrate a story of where I am and what tastes so good. A coffee in the sunshine while skimming through the papers or your favourite book, gathering my children around our kitchen table, which feels smaller every day as they all grow bigger, a crab sandwich looking out across the water, whether on a boat or watching the world go by on the harbour wall, seaside soirées, cooking over fire, watching the sun disappear into the sea, the excitement of a long Sunday lunch, the comfort of preparing the vegetables and the nostalgia of the gravy, all the moments that happen in the kitchen: planning, discussing, debating, chopping, whisking, stirring, beating, roasting, folding, tasting, sharing and, of course, eating.

I love nothing more than heading to the grocer. I become like a child in a sweet shop. Whatever the season, there is always an abundance of ingredients to choose from. Thinking about how we buy produce and what we buy is incredibly important. Find the time to go to your own local grocer, fishmonger, cheese shop, bakery or butcher and support your high street. Small changes made by everyone can ensure a good, positive, sustainable future for us all.

My grandparents gathered around the table in France. Papa in the foreground and Marnie diagonally opposite (wearing a large sun hat) sitting with friends in dappled sunlight underneath the shade of the chestnut trees in the church square in Bagnols-en-Forêt. Papa was always raising a glass. This is one of my favourite places. I can smell the air, feel the sun on my face, hear the buzz of the market and the French gossip of the day. Sharing a table, being together, there is simply nothing better.

Gather

(ALL IN THE DETAILS)

One of my favourite things is to bring people together around the table. Sharing good food, good wine and conversation. I believe this can be achieved very simply, working on the basis that less is more. Like my food, I always go for this approach when styling my home or table, from the choice of guests (who do I want to spend time with in my home) to the basics of setting the table (cut flowers and herbs from the garden) to creating an ambience (the sound of music, candlelight). Turning off the Wi-Fi in my house is an instant way of mustering my children into the same room within minutes (actually, this works for anyone, not just children).

I am a person who loves being sociable but also craves time by myself. Whenever I am in that sociable place, I have so much energy and creativity. Running a restaurant, I suppose I am throwing lunches and suppers every day, so it never feels like a chore to cook for friends or the ones I love. Over the years, I have learned to work fast and be incredibly organised and always seem to have a back-up plan, a just-in-case plan, which of course involves food. I am always prepared for unexpected guests – although it is not something I spend a lot of time thinking about, generally I am. A couple of good bottles are always in the refrigerator. Preserves, too. I always have fresh bread, leaves and whatever is in season from the market, so I can easily produce a warm salad or puff pastry tart. As I write, asparagus is just coming into season, so it is roasted in the oven with a quick mayonnaise and there is supper right there.

The one-pot dishes in the My Kitchen Table chapter (page 82) are a wonderful way of eating together. Another chapter I would love you to make time for is Time to Preserve (page 222). Making jams and jellies may feel like a tiresome task, but with a little thought and organisation, I promise you will not look back.

Coastal Style

(MY STYLE EDIT)

A perfect escape from the world, my life in Cornwall could be drawn from lines in a Daphne du Maurier story. My home reflects a life by the sea and all that brings. White-washed walls with a stripped-back feel, laid-back and vintage, with a pretty garden for outdoor living when not on the beach, it is relaxed and understated, with original artworks, wooden mirrors, faded nautical maps and built-in bookshelves filled with enough to read for days on end. Linens and soft, off-white fabrics, Cornish blankets (made by Atlantic), sea grass and stripped wooden floors add to the lived-in, homely feel. My log-burning stove is for wild-weather evenings curled up on the sofa: woollen socks, a cup of tea, a favourite piece of cake. The bedrooms are simple and feel calm and peaceful. My bathroom has a roll-top bath, white towels and tiled floors, seaweed prints and coastal nods. Much in my home feels classic, with simple pared-back beauty.

French shopping baskets fill my hallway on wooden pegs. These are market buys made over the years, some slightly more worn than others, and always a necessary purchase when I am in France. I use them for so many things and have one for every occasion, for popping into my grocer or heading to the beach for a swim, for picnics, or they are perfect for storage: favourite blankets, glassware, candles and storm lanterns.

Then the greatest room of all – my kitchen. Small but practical and beautifully formed, my kitchen is a creative haven, filling pockets of time throughout the year. It is a place that hugs you on the coldest of days. There is ample storage and a sink with views of the ever-changing seasons. My much-loved wooden table is perfectly sized for every activity, from that early morning quiet cup of tea to a lively supper party with friends, and is covered with paint and scrawlings of words from my children over the years. My shelves are full of essentials and memories, from jars of risotto rice, pastas, lentils, jams, honeys, to sea glass or flowers from my summer garden or autumn and winter foliage, alongside photograph memories, travel buys and seashells from other shores, favourite art – all make my kitchen a brighter place to be.

I keep my larder and – by extension – my refrigerator in order, with dry stores, seeds, nuts and spices (saffron, always), eggs, butter, Cornish sea salt, Parmesan, good olive oil, lemons, crème fraîche and clotted cream always in store, so that I can make a cake, some biscuits or a focaccia at any time. From my kitchen garden are herbs throughout the year, which lift any recipe.

My kitchen – and increasingly my garden – are the places where I feel happiest (my children are in amazement about this, as I am renowned for not being green-fingered). The kitchen, my kitchen, is where you are guaranteed good food. I have said this many times, but there really is nothing better than cooking for the ones you love.

Home Goods

(MY WORKROOM ESSENTIALS)

Magimix gelato ice-cream maker

Just so good. I love making ice cream and sorbets, whatever the weather. This is so easy to use, it makes ice cream, sorbet or gelato in just 30 minutes, which means I can be spontaneous throughout the seasons, whether I have picked an abundance of blackberries in the autumn or I'm making my raspberry ripple ice cream (see page 178) in the summer.

KitchenAid mixer

I could not be without this in my kitchens, both the professional one in my restaurant or the domestic one I have at home (candy pink and nicknamed Mimi). They do far more than just mix – I completely love the pasta attachment.

Cornishware

I love this iconic British design. The classic blue and white stripe of these pieces embody all the nostalgia of growing up for me – a symbol of comfort, love and feeling warm and safe. Leaning into the Aga, kettle on, tea time, any time, there is a piece for my favourite cake, bowl of soup, stacks of plates or pouring cream.

Le Creuset

Cast-iron essentials. My familiar and much-loved Le Creuset dishes are used constantly, from the flint-grey round casseroles to my teal-coloured oval casserole (my one-pot supper dish). Something to pass down the generations. I will always use these pans and I particularly love the new meringue colour range – so classy.

Falcon Enamelware

For beach days, on the boat and home, I love all the colours that each design brings to my kitchen. Teapots, jugs, colanders, mugs, pinch pots, roasting sets and baking sets, I have them all. Joyful.

Coastal Colour

(BODY & SOUL)

I am in the mood for colour, always. I touched on colour in my opening chapter – the palette of sea blues and alexander greens all bright in the always changing Cornish light. Colour is important to me, because much of what I think and feel comes to me in different colours. I draw inspiration in my everyday life from the colour of the ever-changing coastline – the hues that are associated with the seasons that paint the pictures of our lives at different times of year. I was born in July, so I am very much a summer baby, but I love the cooler months of the year – the autumnal colours that gently draw us into the winter months: mustard yellow (or tarky, as we call it in Cornwall), greens and pinks, the greys and blues, so many tones I could not count them. A pop of colour can bring me so much happiness, from the styling of my home to what I cook in my kitchen, in what I wear, even in a new lipstick, colour brings energy and lifts my spirits.

In cooking, colour is essential. You eat with your eyes first. Yes, the food must taste delicious, but the first look is always the most important. The presentation on the plate and the colours are what you appreciate first before moving on to taste, flavour and texture. This year sees the return of block colours in fashion. I love watching the changing trends and being inspired. Just like the fashion world, the food scene is ever-changing and fast-paced, but what I want to do is stand firm with what I love and how I cook (and I do this in what I choose to wear, too). Colour gives energy, but I tend to a base of neutrals and essentials and slowly build towards colour, ultimately creating a beautiful, gentle sense of effortless living and quiet confidence (never arrogance).

Moments in my kitchen are always captured in colour: in the ingredients that I love, which appear each season and fill my larder, in the different times of day and what they feel and smell like, it is colours that appear in my thoughts and inspire me. Throughout this book is a colour wheel of moments in time. I want to draw you in and inspire you to bring colour into your life, too.

Wilds of the Coast & My Kitchen Garden

Sea herbs and flowers are always part of my everyday life. A daze of colour and wonder whatever the season. Bulbs in spring, flowers in summer and a blaze of burnished golds in the autumn. The scent of the garden, a grassy cobbled courtyard, my outside space for gathering is almost as important as inside to me. I have a large faded wooden table for al fresco eating, as well as a firepit and built-in pizza oven for entertaining outside on warm summer nights. Festoon lights and hazel borders bring my indoor style outside.

I have, over the years, become better at growing and really enjoy planning and plotting what to grow in my garden, with the goal of picking, cooking and eating it all. My garden is sheltered and the light is amazing – the coastal flowers and plants thrive in this almost Mediterranean environment. It is important that my garden feels creative with a sense of magic connected to it, giving me a different headspace, a refuge from my everyday life, a place where I can grow, write, cook or bask in the sunshine. Gardening and cooking are so connected and I love the process – all the senses and more: colour, flavour, seasonality, planning and consideration. Composting is a new thing to me and I delight in growing everything from seed to sustain me.

An orchard of trees grows at our house at Harlyn. Apple, plum, pear and quince bring us a harvest in the autumn. Set back from the sea and protected by a crop of woodland, by autumn it really is a treasure trove of goodies. To me, our orchard feels like a place to gather, a focal point and somewhere people and nature seem to just work together. There is also my ever-beautiful fig tree. No blooms as such and harvested according to their own time, the fig is one of my most favourite fruits. I always pick ripe figs for breakfast, salads, tarts, puddings and jams with much excitement. I use the leaves and infuse them in milk and cream for the most delicate coconut flavour in my panna cotta. So clever and delicious. You need a sheltered, sun-drenched wall and perhaps some luck to grow a fig, preferring a slighter cooler climate compared to warmer climes.

As the earth slowly wakes from the long Cornish winter, sea herbs appear, familiar and comforting. Foraging for them is a joy. Beautiful, delicious and rich in vitamins and minerals, my favourites are sea purslane, rock samphire and sea beets. There is so much to appreciate – the wonders of nature. A note on foraging: know what you are looking for and if you are not sure make sure you find out from someone who does.

From May to October, the Cornish coast is carpeted with a variety of colourful wildflowers, in the month of June in particular. Gathered along the coastal path, bringing colour and scent throughout the year, you can find so many examples of native wildflowers. This is part of the reason why this stretch of coastline is both an Area of Outstanding Natural Beauty and a Heritage Coast Area, cared for by The National Trust.

Overleaf, I describe a selection of some of my favourite easy-to-spot Cornish coastal wildflowers...

TAMARISK

These beautiful trees that thrive by the sea remind me of the Mediterranean, framing the edges of the cliffs like a postcard from Provence. Tamarisk blooms through the spring and into summer and is well known for its feathery, pale pink flowers. Ideal for seaside gardens, thanks to wind and salt resistance, it often grows wild and self-sows, but you can also plant it yourself. We recently planted two trees in our garden, so I can look at them every day from my kitchen table.

ROCK SEA SPURREY

Rock sea spurrey is a perennial herb, a mass of leaves and flowers and a pop of purple and pink colour. Salt loving and happy on the open lands down to the sea, it is mostly found growing on coastal cliffs and rocks. From May to October it brings colour and happiness to the coastal paths.

CORNISH (OR ENGLISH) STONECROP

A hardy succulent with small star-shaped white flowers that appear in the summer months, it grows among rocky places such as stone walls and cliff faces.

RED VALERIAN

I am so fond of this plant with dense reddish-pink flowers that appears everywhere, thriving inland and by the sea. From late spring to October it lines the way for us all, in stone walls, fields and cliffs. Bees and butterflies always fall for it, as do moths. There is nothing quite like the month of May and through June where the beautiful landscape is awash with its colour.

SPRING SQUILL

Blue, oh so blue, some say bluer than bluebells. These beautiful plants thrive where the Atlantic winds beat the cliffs, covering the headlands in a wave of blue, six-petalled flowers. They can be found on many exposed cliffs or coastal grasslands shrugging off all the Cornish weather from May to September.

GORSE

A symbol of love and fertility, known also in Cornwall as furze, the sight of this wave of bright yellow flowers appearing all over the county is so familiar, comforting and uplifting. Gorse is perhaps not as friendly as the gentle coconut-and-almond-scented flowers suggest. The dense foliage has gnarly spikes, so it is used as natural hedgerows and a haven for wildlife and shelter for small animals. I only ever want the delicate blooms for salads or infusing into syrups or fudge.

ALEXANDERS

Reaching for the sky, taller and more beautiful than ever, I love the familiar sight of alexanders making their yearly return. Every part is edible (although you must be certain you have the right plant – if you are not 100% sure, do not eat it). The young stems have a similar taste and texture to asparagus and celery except more floral. Trim the stems and roast in the oven with olive oil and sea salt. I always bring in the tall stems in the autumn, dried out from the summer sun. They are simply beautiful arranged in a glass vase.

COWSLIPS

Sunshine yellow. There is something beautifully old-fashioned about the cowslip and how it quietly appears with no fuss or faff among the other wildflowers, with its gently nodding ways. A relative of the primrose, it really does bring me joy, just simply joy.

RAPESEED

Fields of gold. The countryside is ablaze when this sunshine yellow crop appears in spring, signalling that winter is behind us. Rapeseed makes a variety of products, in particular edible oil for cooking – with earthy and nutty undertones it really is delicious. Homegrown, it is our very own olive oil.

SEA PINKS

For me, sea pinks have always hailed the arrival of warmer months, leaving the long winter behind. Also known as Thrift, their lollipop pink flowers are one of Cornwall's most distinctive coastal blooms and folklore suggests that you will never be poor if this plant grows in your garden. I have always loved these hardy candyfloss pink flowers that appear in clusters all over the cliffs in May to September. I even once owned a shop in Port Isaac called Sea Pinks, one of my first businesses in my late twenties, selling coastal style and gifts.

SEA CAMPION

Also known as Dead Man's Bells, Witches' Thimbles and Devil's Hatties, folklore tells us not to pick campion for fear of imminent death, probably due to the flowers growing on the side and edges of cliffs. June to August, this small white-flowered plant grows on cliffs and rocky shingle.

DAISY, DAISY
(GIVE ME YOUR ANSWER DO)

The Ox-eye Daisy is beautiful and a flower I can always identify. A typical grassland flower, like daisies, but bigger. Also known as Moon Daisy or Dog Daisy, this distinctive bloom can be found around the coast and on roadside verges and roundabouts from June to September. The largest native member of the daisy family, it brightens up every day and is beautiful as a simple table arrangement.

WILD SEA FENNEL

A very tall plant in the carrot family with an umbel-type flower similar to dill, coriander and caraway. They have beautiful yellow flowers with a distinct aniseed fragrance, from which fennel pollen is harvested. The flowers are beneficial to bees and butterflies, so are good to have around. Wild fennel does not produce an edible bulb, but its fronds and flowers can be used in the kitchen. Found on dry soil, and my favourite spot at Rock beach overlooking the estuary, from July to October. I love to make fennel blossom ice cream (a recipe that can be found in my first book, *Sea & Shore*).

Rise

Shine

&

(EARLY BIRD)

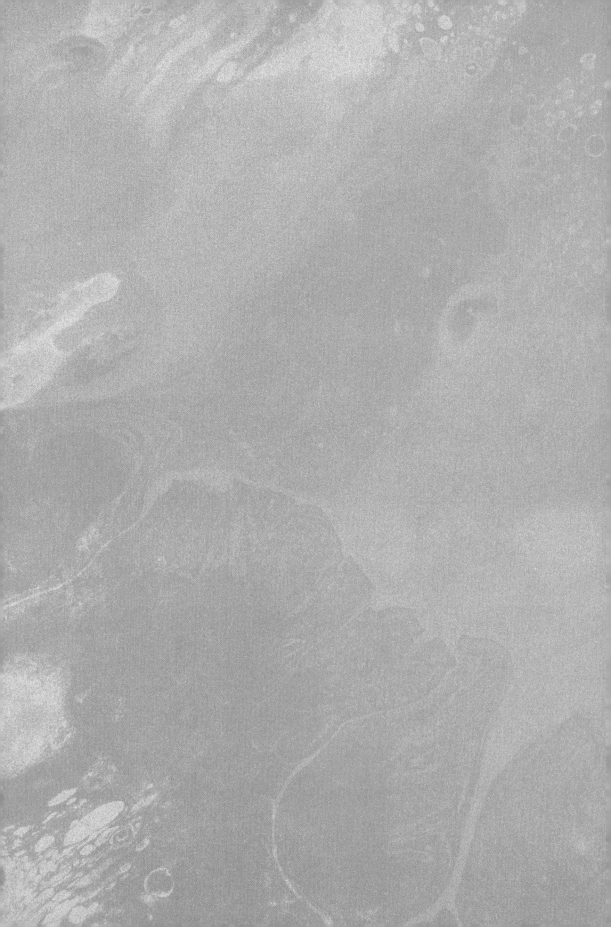

MORNING, golden, red skies as the sun rises. Come rain or shine, I am an early bird. I have never been someone to sleep in or waste the daylight. I am always up and out. (That said, I love my bed and happily go to bed early, which has not often gone hand in hand with restaurant life.) Every morning, I head to the seaside with Inca, my spaniel. This grounds me. In fact, at any time of day, I simply love it, whatever the weather.

Time interests me, as we live in a world that seems as if it is constantly turning at a faster and faster pace. It is sometimes hard to keep up with it, as we increasingly share the details of our lives, often to compare and despair. For me, the early start to my day creates a window of time for myself, for no one else. It's just me and the ocean, and I can really bring my focus back to what I have to do during the coming day without looking too far ahead. The elements around me, from the gentle sunrises of the summer months to the darker, bleaker winter days (all of which I love in their own way), have a certain colour palette and the changing tones of each day give me creative energy, as a cook and beyond.

In this chapter, I want to bring you a sense of well-being and enthusiasm for your own day ahead, bringing you some of my favourite recipes for the early hours, all ideal to fuel your day. From my get-ahead oats to a quick and simple smoothie, or the comforts of crumpets or pancakes for when you have more time, and not forgetting the joy of an omelette, which can be made at any time of the day.

Overnight Oats with Berries & Coconut Milk

Good food should not feel like a chore, it should be a part of your daily routine. A ritual for some self love, to nourish yourself, to sustain a busy life. Overnight oats are perfect sustenance – delicious and easily adapted to whatever you have in your larder at home. I sometimes make this in individual jam jars, as the recipe is enough to make two.

SERVES 2 (OR MAKES 2 X 270 ML/9 FL OZ JAM JARS)

- 100 g (3½ oz/1 cup) porridge (rolled) oats
- 100 g (3½ oz/⅔ cup) blueberries, plus extra to serve
- 150 ml (5 fl oz/scant ⅔ cup) coconut and almond milk, plus extra to serve
- 2 tablespoons honey
- 4 tablespoons plain yoghurt, plus extra to serve
- ½ teaspoon sea salt

TOPPINGS
(see Cook's note)

In a mixing bowl, combine the oats, blueberries, milk, honey, yoghurt and salt. Stir well, then cover (or spoon into individual jars) and place in the refrigerator overnight.

In the morning, you can feel very pleased with yourself as you open the refrigerator to find this readymade goodness. Divide between bowls (unless you have made it in jars), spoon in an extra dollop of yoghurt and a splash of milk, and stir. Sprinkle with your favourite toppings.

COOK'S NOTE Toppings can be anything you love, really: toasted hazelnuts or other nuts, bee pollen, coconut flakes, gorse flowers or other edible flower petals, seasonal berries ... Whatever you choose, your day will be fuelled by goodness.

Old-Fashioned Pancakes, Crispy Bacon & Maple Syrup

This recipe is always made in our house on weekends, school holidays or birthdays. Made with only a few basic ingredients, that you will probably already have in your fridge or larder. Maple syrup is always my go-to topping for rashers of crispy bacon, but of course you can make this your own. Eat with berries, hazelnut butter, raspberry butter or slices of banana and chocolate sauce.

SERVES 4

8 rashers of unsmoked bacon
100 ml (3½ fl oz/scant ½ cup) maple syrup, to serve

FOR THE PANCAKES
350 ml (12 fl oz/generous 1⅓ cups) milk
2 medium free-range eggs, at room temperature
200 g (7 oz/1⅔ cups) plain (all-purpose) flour
2 teaspoons baking powder
a pinch of salt
1 teaspoon sugar
vegetable oil, for frying

Preheat the oven to 200°C (180°C fan/400°F/Gas 6) or the grill (broiler) to high.

Place the bacon on a baking tray and cook in the oven for 15–20 minutes until crispy. Alternatively, grill (broil) until crispy, turning as needed.

For the pancakes, whisk the milk and eggs in a jug, then set aside. Sift the flour and baking powder into a bowl, add a pinch of salt and the sugar, and stir to combine. Make a well in the middle and gradually pour in the milk and egg mixture, whisking well to combine. Be careful not to over-whisk. Leave to rest for 10–15 minutes in the refrigerator.

Brush a non-stick frying pan (skillet) with some vegetable oil, wiping any excess away with paper towels, and set over a medium heat. When the pan is hot, pour about 2 tablespoonfuls of batter into the pan to form a pancake that is about 10 cm (4 in) in diameter. Cook until bubbles start to form in the surface, then flip the pancake over and cook on the other side until golden. Keep warm in a low oven while you repeat with the rest of the batter.

Serve the pancakes immediately with the crispy bacon and drizzled with the maple syrup.

COOK'S NOTES Use the freshest ingredients possible and check the 'use by' dates on your baking powder. Don't worry if the first pancake is not perfect, this always happens. These are thick pancakes, but for thinner pancakes just reduce the milk quantity to 250 ml (8½ fl oz/1 cup), the flour to 100 g (3½ oz/generous ¾ cup) and omit the baking powder. These would have to be topped with lemon and sugar, for me, or made as Crêpes Suzette (what a classic!).

Pictured with The Good Life Berry Smoothie (recipe on page 46).

The Good Life Berry Smoothie

My house is always busy with constantly hungry teenagers – well, young adults, actually – who come and go, so smoothies are always a good idea. There is also something very nourishing about setting apart some time to make your morning smoothie. We always take turns to make them, whether it's a summer's day or a darker morning in the colder months, changing up the ingredients to suit our mood. A smoothie for me has to be very cold, so I always use frozen berries, and I like a thicker consistency. The coconut milk in here is delicious and a good way of letting it down.

SERVES 4

400 g (14 oz) frozen red berry mix
250 g (9 oz) plain yoghurt
a squeeze of honey
1 small ripe banana
50 ml (1¾ fl oz/3 tablespoons) coconut milk, or as needed

Place all of the ingredients in a powerful blender and blitz until smooth. You may want to add some more coconut milk, if you like it a little thinner in consistency.

COOK'S NOTE With the exception of the frozen berries, I always gather my ingredients ready on a tray in the refrigerator the night before, so I find it less of a chore the next morning when I arrive in my kitchen and my smoothie is already halfway there.

Pictured on page 45.

Omelette, Keen's Cheddar, Chives

'Find something you are passionate about and keep tremendously interested in it.' – Julia Child

Like many people, I am inspired by Julia Child, the American cooking teacher, television personality and author. I love her warmth and generous spirit. She loved to learn and never rested on her laurels. Julia's open curiosity, love for food and passion for cooking made her such a star. *Mastering the Art of French Cooking* volumes one and two are the most wonderful books. They transport me straight back to my days spent in France. Homemade mayonnaise, the perfect Poulet Roti, crème Anglaise, puff pastry, that Boeuf Bourguignon with red wine and, of course, the wonderful humble omelette. Julia Child died in 2004, but her legacy remains and she continues to be such an inspiration to so many people around the world. A truly epic, kind-hearted, wonderful woman.

Omelette is perfect for a lazier start to the day and we always have it for breakfast on the warmer days of the year, eaten outside. It is also one of our go-to lunches or easy suppers. The wonder of eggs and all they do.

SERVES 1

- 2 medium free-range eggs, at room temperature
- 15–20 g (½–¾ oz) unsalted butter
- 25 g (1 oz) Keen's Cheddar (or similar), grated
- a handful of chives, snipped
- Cornish sea salt and freshly ground black pepper

Crack the eggs into a bowl and whisk to combine, then season with a good pinch of sea salt and black pepper.

On the stove, melt the butter in a small non-stick frying pan (that favourite pan) or skillet, add the eggs and tilt to spread the mixture out evenly over the base of the pan. As the eggs begin to firm up, but are still a little runny, add most of the grated cheese and chives. Use a spatula to go round the sides of the omelette and fold over in half. Cook for a further 1–2 minutes until golden brown, then gently slide onto a plate and sprinkle with the remaining cheese and chives.

Eat with a smile.

COOK'S NOTE Served on toasted, buttered sourdough, this is my kind of breakfast. Chopped parsley or chevil can replace the chives, or all three chopped together are delicious.

Crumpets

Comfort eating. Buttery crumpets transport me back to cold smoky mornings, spreading generous amounts of salted butter on my Aga-toasted crumpets and watching the butter disappear through the holes. A squeeze of honey, a hot mug of tea, and my day is set. Equally good at tea time or, in fact, any time.

MAKES 12

300 ml (10 fl oz/1¼ cups) whole milk
60 ml (2 fl oz/¼ cup) water
1 teaspoon caster (superfine) sugar
1 tablespoon fast-action dried yeast
225 g (8 oz/1¾ cups) strong plain (bread) flour
1 teaspoon sea salt
vegetable oil, for greasing and cooking

Heat the milk and water together in a small saucepan until lukewarm, then pour into a jug. Stir in the sugar and dried yeast, then leave in a warm place for 10–15 minutes until there is a good frothy head on the mixture.

Meanwhile, sift the flour and salt into a mixing bowl and make a well in the middle. When the yeast mixture is frothy, pour it all in. Use a whisk to gradually work the flour into the liquid, then beat well at the end to make a perfectly smooth batter. Cover the bowl with a clean dish towel and leave to stand in a warm place for about 45 minutes until the batter has become light and frothy.

To cook the crumpets, grease the insides of your crumpet rings (see Cook's note) well, then grease the frying pan (skillet) before placing it over a medium heat. Arrange the rings in the frying pan. When the pan is hot, spoon 1 tablespoon of the crumpet batter into each ring. Let them cook for 4–5 minutes: first, tiny bubbles will appear on the surface and then, suddenly, they will burst, leaving the traditional holes. Carefully lift off the rings and turn the crumpets over. Cook the crumpets on their second sides for about 1 minute only, then remove from the pan.

Re-grease and reheat the rings and pan before cooking the next batch of crumpets. Keep warm in a low oven. If making them ahead of time, toast the crumpets lightly on each side before serving.

COOK'S NOTE A little like a pancake, the first crumpet you cook can feel disappointing. Do not fear, they get better and better. Use metal crumpet rings or pastry cutters to cook them (available from all good cook shops).

Dippy Egg & Cornish Asparagus, Soldiers

Hooray for soldiers, so many options: toasted sourdough; rarebit; pigs in blankets; smothered in anchovy butter (so comforting); and, of course, a favourite of mine – these delicious green spears of wonder. Asparagus has a very short season, so I would encourage you to eat as much as possible in pancakes, pasta, tarts, raw in salads, risotto and soups. The options are plentiful.

SERVES 2

- 2 free-range eggs, at room temperature
- 6 asparagus spears
- 1 tablespoon good olive oil
- sourdough loaf, for toasting
- butter, for spreading
- Cornish sea salt and freshly ground black pepper

Preheat the oven to 200°C (180°C fan/400°F/Gas 6).

Bring a medium saucepan of water to the boil. Make sure your eggs are at room temperature. Slowly lower the eggs into the water and cook for 4–5 minutes for dippy, or 6–7 minutes for soft.

Trim the asparagus, place on a baking tray (pan), drizzle with the olive oil and season with sea salt. Roast in the oven for 6–8 minutes, depending on the thickness of the spears.

Meanwhile, slice your sourdough loaf and toast.

Serve the eggs in your favourite egg cups, seasoned with salt and freshly ground black pepper. Spread a generous amount of butter on your toast and slice into soldiers, then serve alongside the asparagus.

COOK'S NOTE Store asparagus like you would freshly cut flowers: trim the bottoms and stand upright in a jug of water. My kind of blooms – eat in abundance, when in season.

Figgy Banana Bread

Ripe, beautiful figs, sunk into golden syrupy banana bread ... Although it IS cake, when toasted with butter, it can definitely turn into breakfast. I will never tire of banana bread – sometimes, it is all you need. There are so many variations out there, but this recipe is definitely a favourite of mine.

SERVES 6

- 125 g (4 oz) salted butter, softened, plus extra for greasing
- 4 large ripe bananas
- 250 g (9 oz/2 cups) self-raising (self-rising) flour
- 200 g (7 oz/scant 1 cup) caster (superfine) sugar
- 3 medium free-range eggs
- 4 tablespoons golden syrup
- 3 fresh figs: 2 chopped into small pieces; 1 sliced

Preheat the oven to 200°C (180°C fan/400°F/Gas 6). Butter a 450 g (1 lb) loaf tin (pan) and line with baking parchment.

In a food processor, blend the bananas, then add all the other ingredients, except the figs. Blend again, then scrape down the sides and mix through.

Pour the batter into a bowl and gently fold in the chopped figs. Spoon the mixture into the buttered tin and place the slices of fig along the top of the mixture.

Bake for 1½ hours, covering the top with foil after 45 minutes, until a skewer inserted into the centre comes out clean. Leave to rest for 10 minutes, then turn out onto a cooling rack.

Serve warm. Toasted with butter is delicious, too.

COOK'S NOTE This will keep in an airtight container for 3 days and also freezes well.

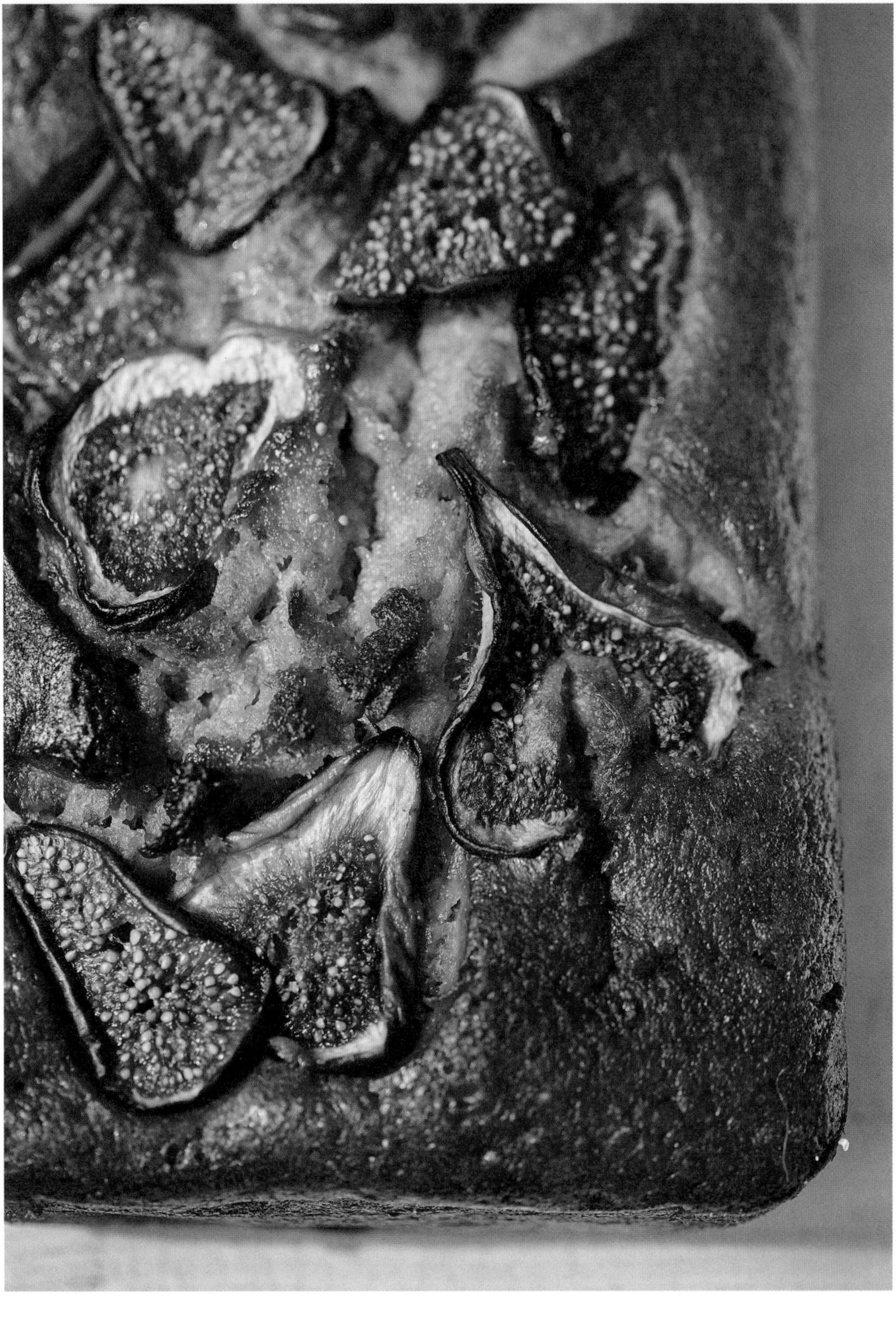

Fruit Salad with Elderflower Syrup & Garden Mint

Sometimes I just crave a fruit salad, so it's always a good thing to have in the refrigerator ready to go. I keep a fruit salad in my fridge and it never lasts long. The key is to just stir in enough syrup to gently sweeten it rather than overpower the natural sweetness of the fruit, and to use lots of fresh mint. You can adapt to your favourite fruits. Lifts any day.

SERVE 4

½ pineapple, chopped into bite-size pieces
2 kiwi fruit, peeled and sliced
1 punnet of raspberries
1 punnet of strawberries, hulled and halved
1 mango, peeled, stoned and chopped into bite-size pieces
50 g (2 oz) fresh mint

FOR THE SYRUP
2–3 tablespoons elderflower cordial
freshly squeezed juice of 2 oranges

Prepare all the fruit and combine in a bowl. Finely chop or tear the fresh mint as you prefer and add to the fruit.

Combine the syrup ingredients, then pour 2–3 tablespoons of the syrup over the fruit and gently fold through.

COOK'S NOTE Although fruit is available all year round, in my view it is always better to eat what's in season and at its best. That means strawberries in June and blackberries in September. A lovely way of enjoying fruits throughout the year is to freeze them in small batches, to use in crumbles, pies, galettes, or in your morning smoothie (see page 46).

Provence – Bagnols-en-Forêt 83600

(OH LA LA)

Close your eyes and click your ruby slippers together three times and let me transport you to one of the places in my life that means so much to me. I touched on my connections between France and Cornwall in my first book, *Sea & Shore*. Papa, my grandfather was half-French, so there was always a strong French influence in my life. My second book could not be without a nod to those roots and the influence they had on me, both in cooking and life in general.

I want you to imagine my days spent with Papa, as we called my grandfather. Provençal summer sunshine, pine trees, a dusty mountain road, bouncing around in the back of a classic yellow D5 Citroën as we wound our way up to the village of Bagnols-en-Forêt, located in the foothills of the Massif de l'Esterel, its climate softened by a salty sea breeze. I have known this peaceful place my entire life. Papa would drive me and my sister Harriet to collect milk for breakfast. We were only allowed to come away with the milk if we asked the farmer for it in French. I vividly remember the slight fear that would come over me and the butterflies in my tummy as we approached the farm, practising: *Je voudrais du lait s'ils vous plait. Je voudrais du lait s'ils vous plait.* I can remember the smell of the leather seats in the car and the warm air as it hit our faces as we leaned out of the windows in anticipation. Triumphantly, we did it! We would arrive back at our villa, Les Levriers, with smiles on our faces, feeling victorious. My grandmother, Marnie, would have breakfast laid out on the terrace: a table cloth, freshly squeezed orange juice, set yoghurts, croissants, French bread, every confiture possible and Provençal honey, always with a busy bunch of wasps competing for the jams. White peaches, apricots and melon from the melon man, who would arrive with great enthusiasm on the dusty road outside the villa. All the senses filled with the beautiful fragrance from the mountainside lavender, rosemary and pine.

'Á table'. This was often heard and we would all come rushing together around the kitchen table. It was a natural thing for my family to do, a place to gather to share our day and the food was always a highlight. Papa would be there talking to us in Franglais. He was the most amazing man, a gentleman. He would always greet you with three kisses to the cheeks and then quietly say, '*courage*' ('have courage', in French). This is something that has stayed with me forever. Water and wine (as children, this was always cause for excitement). Watching Papa as he poured the grape juice into our glasses, swirling it, looking at the colour,

using all the senses. Cheese eaten before pudding to finish the red wine. A siesta was always part of our day – an hour in the shade away from the burning sunshine. Papa would wake us up from this (not that we ever went to sleep) by throwing French sweets onto our beds. As children, there was always much excitement at this.

We would spend exciting days meandering through the markets discovering nature's seasonal offerings, tasting honey, cheese, charcuterie. The colours, the energy, the buzz. The Provençal flair was mesmerising.

Spending so much time in France from my early years and throughout my life has inspired me and contributed to how I feel today about the importance of a table and bringing people together. Those were carefree, beautiful days, which hold such vivid memories for me. One day, given the oppurtunity, I hope to bring the elements of my time spent in France – the people, the places, the stories, the recipes – together in another book. Until then ...

Petit déjeuner with my grandparents, Marnie and Papa, my mother Lucy and sister Harriet, in Bagnols-en-Forêt, 1977.

Morning

Café

(GENTLY DOES IT)

POLLEN yellow, zesty yellow, all the yellows that radiate warmth and energy. I never want to miss this time of day. It is well known that in Cornwall we 'rush slowly' – here, life feels as if it is moving at a slower pace than in the city. We like to stop for 'crib time', which means a mid-morning snack in North Cornwall, or 'croust' as it is called further west. Whether I am busy in my restaurant or having a slower start to my morning, my mid-morning break for coffee and 'crib' is a favourite time of day. It's a pick-me-up, a reboot, or perhaps just a pleasurable habit of routine. It might take the form of a meet-up with friends, or a date with Mark over a *café*, or one those creative business meetings that bring like-minded people together, but whether I am working or simply pottering about, coffee time always brings me the greatest joy. For me, I always need always something sweet to go with it. The recipes in this chapter make me feel nostalgic, from the celebration cake to just the shortest shortbread to indulging in a doughnut or saffron buns. Life is sweet in every way.

Rose-Petal Shortbread

Shortbread is always a favourite – a classic biscuit that I love at teatime. The wonder at the clever short layers dusted with caster sugar is always such a treat. Rose petals are quite pungent, but add a lovely fragrance to the biscuit. They are also delicious dipped in white chocolate and pistachios, if you would like to be more indulgent. The dough freezes well, as do the biscuits once they are baked.

MAKES ABOUT 12 PIECES

- 200 g (7 oz) unsalted butter, softened
- 100 g (3½ oz/scant ½ cup) soft light brown sugar
- 3 teaspoons dried rose petals, plus extra for decorating
- ½ teaspoon rose water
- 300 g (10½ oz/scant 2½ cups) plain (all-purpose) flour, plus extra for dusting
- 2 tablespoons golden caster (superfine) sugar, for sprinkling

Preheat the oven to 190°C (170°C fan/375°F/Gas 5) and line a baking sheet with baking parchment.

In a large bowl, beat the softened butter and soft light brown sugar together until pale and smooth. Add the dried rose petals and rose water, then sift over the flour and mix until it comes together into a smooth dough.

Turn out onto a lightly floured surface and use a rolling pin to gently roll out the dough to 1 cm (½ in) thick. Cut into rounds and place on the prepared baking sheet, then sprinkle each round with a little extra sugar. Place the baking sheet in the refrigerator to chill for 15 minutes.

Transfer the sheet of shortbread to the oven and bake for 10–15 minutes until pale golden brown. Transfer to a wire rack to cool and dust with the caster sugar and a few more dried rose petals.

COOK'S NOTES Rose water can overpower so be restrained with it. A heart-shaped cutter is pretty if cooking for a celebration or the one you love. If you would like a more traditional-looking shortbread, bake in a lined 30 x 25 cm (12 x 10 in) traybake tin (pan) and cut the shortbread into fingers or triangles while still in the tin as soon as you remove it from the oven. Swap out the rose petals for lavender sugar and flowers (see page 228).

Golden Saffron Buns

Ode to beautiful saffron. Rich, spiced, yeasty, colour of the sunrise, these buns are sweet with juicy raisins. Ideal for crib time (see page 65) or tea time. Swapping out the butter for clotted cream feels more Cornish. Crib never tasted so good.

MAKES 10

- 250 ml (8½ fl oz/1 cup) milk
- ½ x 1 g pot of saffron (about ½ tablespoon)
- 1 x 113 g (3¾ oz) tub of clotted cream (see Cook's note)
- 500 g (1 lb 2 oz/4 cups) strong white (bread) flour, plus extra for dusting
- 1 teaspoon sea salt
- 50 g (2 oz/scant ¼ cup) caster (superfine) sugar
- 7 g (1 sachet) fast-action dried yeast
- 1½ teaspoons allspice
- 100 g (3½ oz) raisins, soaked for 15–20 minutes in 2 tablespoons Cornish rum (or apple juice if you prefer), then sieved to remove excess liquid

FOR THE GLAZE

- 50 g (2 oz/scant ¼ cup) caster (superfine) sugar
- 2 tablespoons water

Gently heat the milk in a small pan until it's steaming. Add the saffron to the milk and leave to infuse for 20 minutes off the heat.

Add the clotted cream to the saffron-infused milk and return to a low heat for 2–3 minutes. Gently whisk until melted and combined. The mixture should be just warm to the touch.

Sift the flour into a large bowl and stir in the salt, sugar, yeast and allspice. Make a well in the middle of the dry ingredients and pour in the warm milk. Mix and bring together into a soft dough.

Knead the dough on a slow speed in a stand mixer with the dough hook attachment for 7–10 minutes, or by hand on a lightly floured surface, incorporating the sieved raisins after 5 minutes. The dough should bounce back when touched. Place in a bowl, cover and leave in a warm place for 45 minutes–1 hour, or until doubled in size.

Knock back the dough, turn out onto a floured surface and knead briefly. Divide the dough into 10 equal portions (about 100 g/3½ oz) each to make buns and place on a baking sheet lined with baking parchment. Cover the buns and leave to prove again for 30 minutes.

Meanwhile, preheat the oven to 220°C (200°C fan/430°F/Gas 8).

Bake the buns for 25 minutes or until golden.

For the glaze, gently heat the sugar and water in a saucepan until the sugar has dissolved, then boil for 1 minute.

Brush the hot syrup over the warm buns. Transfer to a wire rack and leave to cool.

Serve toasted and spread generously with clotted cream or butter.

COOK'S NOTE I use clotted cream in my saffron buns instead of butter, which works really well, giving a creamy, slightly lighter (if that is possible) texture. If you would prefer to use butter, you can.

Orange-Zested Doughnuts with Lemon Curd

These doughnuts are life enhancing and, of course, easily adapted for any season with different jams, creams and custards. Lemon curd is a winner for me. Can you eat one without licking your lips, that is the question?

MAKES 12

300 g (10½ oz/scant 2½ cups) strong white (bread) flour, plus extra for dusting
3 teaspoons fast-action dried yeast
pinch of Cornish sea salt
55 g (2 oz/½ cup) golden caster (superfine) sugar, plus extra for dusting
2 medium free-range egg yolks
grated zest of 1 orange
175 ml (6 fl oz/¾ cup) tepid water
130 g (4 oz) unsalted butter, softened
1 litre (34 fl oz/4 cups) vegetable oil, for deep-frying
1 x 320 g (11¼ oz) jar of lemon curd

Sift the flour into the bowl of a stand mixer fitted with the paddle attachment. Add the yeast, salt, sugar, egg yolks, orange zest and tepid water. Mix gently on a medium speed for 10 minutes. Continue mixing and add the softened butter, 30 g (1 oz) at a time, until completely incorporated and the dough looks glossy and comes away from the sides of the bowl.

Sprinkle a large bowl with flour, place the dough in it and cover with a clean dish towel. Leave in a warm place for 1 hour, or until doubled in size.

Knock the dough back, then transfer it to a clean bowl, cover and leave in the refrigerator overnight.

The next day, cut the dough into 12 small pieces and roll into balls with floured hands. Place on a baking sheet, evenly spaced. Leave to prove in a warm place for 30 minutes, or until doubled in size.

Half-fill a large deep saucepan with the oil and heat to 170–180°C (340–355°F) or until a cube of bread sizzles and rises to the surface in 30 seconds. Fry the doughnuts in batches of 2–3 at a time until golden brown. Remove with a slotted spoon to drain on paper towels.

Place some extra sugar on a plate nearby, then roll the warm doughnuts in the sugar to finish.

To fill, make a small hole in the side of each doughnut with the end of a narrow wooden spoon handle. Place the lemon curd in a small piping bag and snip off the tip. Pipe a small amount of curd into the hole in each doughnut.

Eat warm, ideally immediately.

COOK'S NOTE Take care while frying and make sure the temperature of the oil stays consistent. The doughnuts will easily burn if the oil is too hot.

Coconut & Jam Sponge

Old-fashioned school tea-time treat (remember raspberry and coconut sponge?). Such nostalgic flavours. I usually serve it with a jug of warm custard, and it makes a quick and easy cake for unexpected guests. Kettle on.

SERVES 6

FOR THE BATTER

225 g (8 oz) unsalted butter, softened, plus extra for greasing
225 g (8 oz/1 cup) golden caster (superfine) sugar
4 medium free-range eggs
225 g (8 oz/1¾ cups) self-raising (self-rising) flour

TO DECORATE

150 g (5 oz/½ cup) raspberry jam (jelly)
100 g (3½ oz/1 generous cup) desiccated (shredded unsweetened) coconut

Preheat the oven to 200°C (180°C fan/400°F/Gas 6). Grease a 25 cm (10 in) square baking tin (pan).

For the batter, I use the all-in-one method, mixing everything together until well combined. Simply place the softened butter, sugar, eggs and flour into a stand mixer fitted with the paddle attachment and beat until pale and fluffy.

Pour the batter into the prepared tin and bake for 15–20 minutes until firm and a skewer inserted into the centre comes out clean.

Allow to cool (be patient).

To decorate, spoon the raspberry jam over the top of the cake and spread evenly, then sprinkle with the coconut. Cut into squares and eat happily.

COOK'S NOTE Apricot jam and toasted almonds make a lovely alternative for the topping. My favourite tin for baking this is a Falcon 25 cm (10 in) square baking tray in pigeon grey.

Coffee & Walnut Cake

I can remember making coffee cake when I was growing up, whenever I wanted to be a little more adventurous. Camp coffee was the thing to use back then (and still is), although I now use Cornish Origin coffee in double shots, which gives a smooth, rich flavour to this nutty, buttery, moreish cake. (Although there is something so good about using Camp coffee now and then, just for the trip down memory lane!)

SERVES 8

FOR THE SPONGES
- 2 tablespoons double-shot espresso
- 250 g (9 oz) unsalted butter, softened
- 250 g (9 oz/generous 1 cup) golden caster (superfine) sugar
- 250 g (9 oz/2 cups) self-raising (self-rising) flour, sifted
- 4 medium free-range eggs, whisked lightly

FOR THE ICING (FROSTING)
- 2 tablespoons double-shot espresso
- 325 g (11 oz/generous 2½ cups) icing (confectioner's) sugar, sifted
- 150 g (5 oz) salted butter

TO DECORATE
- 200 g (7 oz/2 cups) walnut halves

Preheat oven to 200°C (180°C fan/400°F/Gas 6). Line the bases of two loose-bottomed 18 cm (7 in) round cake tins (pans) with baking parchment and lightly butter the sides.

Make the espresso (enough for both sponge and icing) and allow it to cool.

For the sponges, combine the softened butter, sugar, flour, eggs and cooled espresso in a mixing bowl and mix until light and fluffy. Divide the mixture between the two prepared tins and bake in the oven for 20–25 minutes. The sponges are cooked when you lightly press them and they spring back. Allow to cool slightly, then turn out onto a cooling rack to cool completely.

For the icing, place the icing sugar in a mixing bowl with the softened butter and cooled espresso, and beat until light and creamy.

Place most of the walnuts (keep back some halves for decoration) in a food processor and whizz until roughly chopped.

When the sponges are completely cold (be patient), spread 3 tablespoons of the icing over one and sandwich together with the other. I like to ice the whole cake, top and sides, using a small palette knife. Once iced, evenly cover the sides of the cake with the chopped walnuts, pressing them in with the palms of your hands. Garnish the top of the cake with the reserved walnuts and then put the kettle on.

Baby Meringues Sandwiched with Vanilla Cream

I think meringues and cream are one of the best partnerships. Chewy and sweet, rich and pale golden.

MAKES 6-8 SANDWICHED MERINGUES

- 4 large free-range egg whites (save the yolks for making aioli, see page 162)
- 115 g (3¾ oz/½ cup) caster (superfine) sugar
- 115 g (3¾ oz/scant 1 cup) icing (confectioner's) sugar, plus extra for dusting

FOR THE VANILLA CREAM

- 250 ml (8½ fl oz/1 cup) double (heavy) cream
- ½ vanilla pod (bean), split
- 2 tablespoons icing (confectioner's) sugar, sifted

Preheat the oven to 120°C (100°C fan/250°F/Gas ¼). Line a baking sheet with baking parchment.

In a spotlessly clean dry bowl, whisk the egg whites to stiff peaks (the egg whites should stand tall when the whisk is lifted). Very slowly add the caster sugar, a tablespoon at a time, beating for 2–3 seconds between each addition until thick and glossy. Sift in the icing sugar and gently fold in with a metal spoon or spatula. Do not overmix - the meringue should look soft and billowy.

Spoon 12–16 slightly scruffy small mounds of meringue onto the prepared baking sheet and bake for 1½ hours, or until they are crisp and slightly coloured. Turn off the oven and leave to cool in the oven.

When cool, whip the cream. Scrape the seeds from the vanilla pod and add to the cream along with the icing sugar, then fold in.

Sandwich pairs of meringue together with the vanilla cream. Serve dusted with icing sugar.

COOK'S NOTES Fold in 3 tablespoons of lemon curd to make lemon cream. For another variation, crush 100 g (3½ oz) raspberries and fold into the cream. The meringues will keep for 2 weeks in an airtight container. When making meringues, always make sure your utensils are clean and dry. Leftover egg yolks can be used for my Saffron Aioli on page 162.

Clotted Cream & Lemon Drizzle Bundt Cake

Lemons are a winter fruit but always bring yellow sunshine to my kitchen. They are an ingredient I would just not want to be without. This is a perfect cake for any time of the year. Baking is one of the most loving of all human skills, so what better way to show how much you love your mother? So quick and simple, it will brighten up your day. I use a Nordic Ware swirl bundt tin (pan) in which to bake it, which makes this cake a real showstopper for a pudding or afternoon tea.

SERVES 10

FOR THE SPONGE
vegetable oil, for greasing
450 g (1 lb/scant 2 cups) caster (superfine) sugar
4 medium free-range eggs
finely grated zest and juice of 4 lemons
500 g (1 lb 2 oz/2½ cups) clotted cream (I use Rodda's), plus extra to serve
2 tablespoons milk
400 g (14 oz/3¼ cups) self-raising (self-rising) flour

FOR THE LEMON DRIZZLE
zest and juice of 4 lemons
4 tablespoons granulated sugar

TO DECORATE
edible flowers (I like to use primrose when in season)
rosemary sprigs
extra granulated sugar

TO SERVE
dollops of Rodda's clotted cream or a drizzle of pouring cream

For the sponge, preheat the oven to 180°C (160°C fan/350°F/Gas 4). Lightly oil a swirled bundt tin (pan), 25 cm diameter x 9 cm tall (10 x 3½ in).

Beat the caster sugar and eggs in a large bowl until light, fluffy and doubled in size. Set aside.

Grate the zest and squeeze the juice of the lemons into a separate bowl, then add the clotted cream and stir together.

Gently beat the lemony clotted cream into the sugar and eggs, then add the milk and mix in. Sift in the flour, then gently fold it into the mixture until well combined. Spoon the mixture into the prepared tin and level the top.

Bake for 45 minutes–1 hour, or until a skewer inserted into the centre of the cake comes out clean. Remove from the oven and leave to cool in the tin for 10 minutes, before turning out onto a wire rack. After a further 10 minutes, carefully transfer the bundt to your serving plate.

For the lemon drizzle, mix together the lemon zest, juice and granulated sugar in a small pan. Heat gently until the sugar dissolves, then allow to cool.

While the cake is still warm, make little holes in it with a skewer or cocktail stick, then pour the lemon drizzle syrup evenly over the cake. Sprinkle it with more granulated sugar, flowers and herbs to decorate. Cut into slices and serve with extra cream.

COOK'S NOTE 'Bundt' is derived from a German word meaning 'a cake for gathering' – simply perfect.

My

(CHILD-LIKE WONDER)

Table

Kitchen

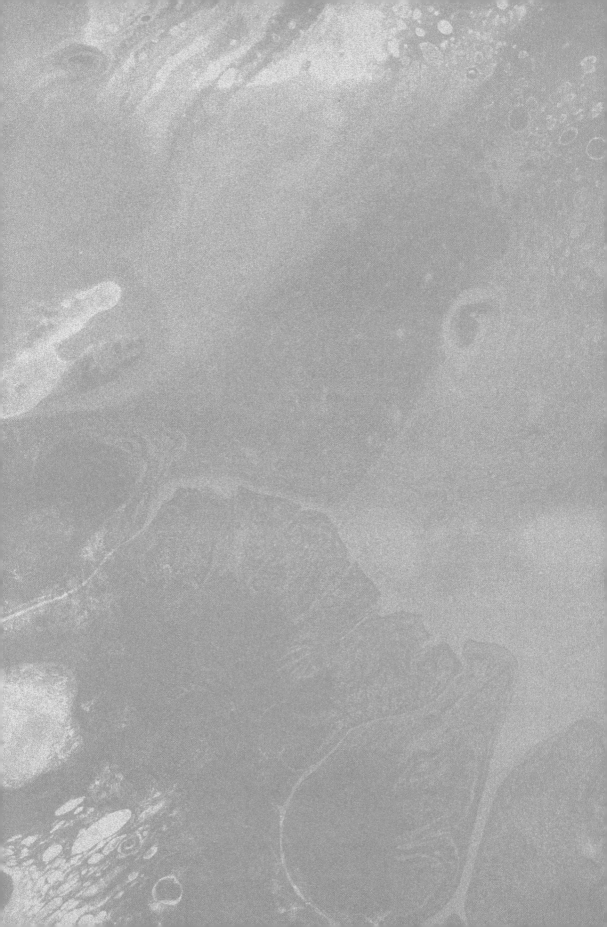

SEA green. As the saying goes, all the best parties end up in the kitchen. The kitchen is the place I am most drawn to – the heart of the house, where you will always find something good to eat. It is a place of rituals, routines and comfort, and always a palace of wonders to me. I can remember unpacking the shopping for my mother as a child, wide-eyed and always hungry, waiting in keen anticipation of what she might have in store. Eating together is and always will be a highlight for me, a little thought and love go a long way. My kitchen is a place for family favourites, spontaneous bakes, breakfast time, testing recipes, boiling the kettle, putting the world to rights, leaning into the Aga on a chilly day, birthdays, high days and holidays ... the kitchen is where life comes alive.

One-pot suppers are very much how we love to eat as a family – one dish placed in the middle of our kitchen table to share as we come together at the end of the day. Time for fish suppers, hearty chicken, the happiness of pasta, crumbles and other childhood favourites, a feeling of comfort and a sense of being grounded and happy. My kitchen is always my safe place.

Pea, Watercress & Mint Soup

Peas. I just love peas, especially paired with another favourite of mine: glorious peppery, green and uplifting watercress. And mint is one herb that is a must in pots outside your kitchen door or simply on a windowsill. Green is for go and the feel-good factor. A quick and easy recipe. Add the watercress and mint for the garnish at the last minute so they do not wilt or discolour.

SERVES 4

- 100 g (3½ oz) unsalted butter
- 2 tablespoons good olive oil
- 2 garlic cloves, thinly sliced
- 1 leek, white part, finely sliced
- 1 potato, peeled and chopped
- 300 g (10½ oz) watercress, plus extra to garnish
- 1.5 litres (50 fl oz/generous 6 cups) chicken or vegetable stock
- 500 g (1 lb 2 oz/scant 4 cups) petit pois
- a small handful of mint, chopped, plus extra to garnish
- 200 g (7 oz/generous ¾ cup) crème fraîche
- Cornish sea salt and freshly ground black pepper

Melt the butter and olive oil in a large saucepan over a medium heat, then add the garlic, leek, potato and watercress and cook until gently softened. Place a cartouche (a circle of greaseproof paper) over the top and leave to gently cook for 10–15 minutes.

Remove the cartouche and add the stock and simmer for 15 minutes, then add the peas and cook for a further 1–2 minutes. Remove from the heat and allow to cool.

Pour the cooled mixture into a food processor or blender (in batches), add the chopped mint and blitz until smooth.

Return the soup to a clean saucepan over a low heat to warm through. Add 4 tablespoons of the crème fraîche and stir in, then season with sea salt and freshly ground black pepper, to taste. Ladle into warm soup bowls and garnish with extra watercress, mint and the remaining crème fraîche.

COOK'S NOTE Versatile watercress is wonderful not only in soups, but also in smoothies, salads, sandwiches and butters.

Evie's Macaroni Cheese (Tabasco a must)

Over the years, if I asked Evie (my daughter) what she would like for supper, there has only ever been one answer: Macaroni Cheese. From a little girl to a young woman, ketchup always, peas probably... but now, with her ever-changing tastes, it is all about a crunchy topping, Tabasco and what cheese. This is how it goes. It's not one for the faint-hearted and certainly a dish you need to eat with abandon.

SERVES 4

2 large thick slices of slightly stale sourdough
80 g (3 oz) Parmesan, grated
grated zest of 1 lemon
500 ml (17 fl oz/2 cups) milk
1 small white onion, quartered
4 black peppercorns
2 bay leaves
whole nutmeg, for grating
300 g (10½ oz) macaroni
30 g (1 oz) unsalted butter
4 tablespoons plain (all-purpose) flour
80 g (3 oz) Cornish Gouda, grated
80 g (3 oz) Keen's Cheddar, grated
2 teaspoons English mustard
Cornish sea salt and freshly ground black pepper
Tabasco sauce, to serve

Whizz the sourdough bread to crumbs in a food processor – you want two good handfuls. Mix the Parmesan and lemon zest with the crumbs and set aside.

Combine the milk, onion, peppercorns, bay leaves and a grating of nutmeg in a saucepan and bring to the boil, then turn off the heat and allow to infuse for 10 minutes. Strain into a jug, discarding the onion, peppercorns and bay leaves.

Meanwhile, bring a large pan of salted water to the boil, add the macaroni and cook for 3 minutes less than stated in the packet instructions. Drain, saving 2 tablespoons of the pasta cooking water.

Melt the butter in a separate large saucepan, and stir in the flour to make a roux of a biscuit-y colour. Remove from the heat and gradually add the still-warm milk, whisking all the time, then place back over a low heat until the sauce thickens. Remove from the heat and add the Gouda, Cheddar and mustard, then stir in the cooked macaroni. Season with sea salt and freshly ground black pepper, to taste. Stir in the reserved pasta water and pour the mixture into a gratin dish. Top with the cheesy zesty breadcrumbs.

Bake for 25 minutes until the top is golden and crunchy.

For a kick, serve with some Tabasco sauce on top. Buttered petit pois always.

COOK'S NOTE It is really worth infusing the milk with onion, nutmeg, peppercorns and bay. This will give you a sauce full of flavour that complements the cheesiness. Warming the milk up also makes for a smoother sauce when adding to the roux.

Roast Chicken with Chorizo, Garlic & Rosemary

There is nothing more comforting than a roast chicken – a go-to every week and something my family are always happy to see. Perhaps it is the nostalgia of Sunday lunches past that always bring us all together with great hunger and happiness. I use a properly free-range Pipers Farm chicken – top birds. The chorizo, lemon and rosemary create a wonderful gravy of buttery golden juices; with the potatoes and garlic, it really is a delicious one-pot recipe.

SERVES 4

- 1 whole properly free-range chicken (about 1.5 kg/ 3 lb 5 oz)
- 50–100 g (2–3½ oz) unsalted butter, softened
- 6 rashers of unsmoked streaky bacon
- 2 lemons, halved
- 8 rosemary sprigs
- 12 garlic cloves, left whole and unpeeled
- 2 tablespoons olive oil
- 300 g (10½ oz) chorizo, thickly sliced
- 500 g (1 lb 2 oz) small new potatoes, left whole
- Cornish sea salt and freshly ground black pepper

Preheat the oven to 200°C (180°C fan/400°F/Gas 6).

Place the chicken in an oven-to-table roasting dish. Rub the breasts and legs with the butter, season with sea salt and freshly ground black pepper, then place the streaky bacon over the breasts of the chicken. (This protects the breast meat for the first part of the cooking, keeping the meat moist and adding delicious flavour. The crispy bacon becomes the cook's perk.) Place the lemon halves and most of the rosemary in the cavity. Arrange the garlic cloves around the chicken in the oven dish, then drizzle the whole chicken with the olive oil.

Roast in the oven for 15–20 minutes until the bacon is crispy.

Remove the dish from the oven, remove the bacon and set aside. Baste the chicken with the buttery and lemony juices, then arrange the slices of chorizo and small potatoes around the chicken with the remaining rosemary sprigs. Return to the oven to roast for 45 minutes–1 hour until the chicken is golden brown and the juices run clear (test by inserting a skewer into a leg).

Remove from the oven and allow to rest for 10 minutes. Carve and serve with the buttery, golden juices, with the roasted potatoes and chorizo, accompanied by greens or a green salad.

COOK'S NOTE Strip the chicken if there are any leftovers. I always make risotto the next day and use the carcass for making a stock.

Chou-fleur Roasted Whole with Tarragon, Butter & Sherry

We love *chou-fleur* – cauliflower – in our house (cauliflower cheese is another favourite) and in recent times baking it whole has gone down particularly well. A one-pot supper that is really easy to prepare ahead and then the oven does all the work. Serve with buttery mash and greens.

SERVES 4

- 1 whole cauliflower
- 250 ml (8½ fl oz/1 cup) chicken stock (or vegetable stock if you prefer)
- 250 ml (8½ fl oz/1 cup) sherry
- 150 g (5 oz) unsalted butter
- 1 bunch of tarragon, leaves only
- 1 tablespoon Dijon mustard
- julienned zest of 1 lemon
- Cornish sea salt and freshly ground black pepper

Trim the cauliflower leaving all the leaves intact.

In a small saucepan, combine the stock, sherry, two-thirds of the butter and half of the tarragon with the mustard and lemon zest, and warm gently.

Place the cauliflower in a deep-sided roasting pan, brush all over with the remaining butter and season with sea salt and black pepper. Pour over the warmed stock mixture and cover in kitchen foil. Roast in the oven for 1 hour, basting the cauliflower every 10–15 minutes. Leave uncovered for the last 15 minutes of cooking until the cauliflower is golden brown and tender (this will depend on the size of the cauliflower – use a skewer or the tip of a knife to check the thickest part).

Carve the cauliflower into 4 quarters, spoon over the buttery juices and garnish with the remaining tarragon. Serve with buttery mash. Dreamy.

COOK'S NOTE Sadly, this humble vegetable was not always showcased to its best back in my school days. I love it now as it goes such a long way. Always remember to cook the leaves – a great way to reduce waste and they are so delicious and pretty.

Cornish Mussels, Smoked Bacon, Cider, Clotted Cream, Wild Garlic

For me, cooking with the ebb and flow of nature makes sense. Cooking seasonally brings me such joy – new ingredients appear and I am always so happy to see them. Wild garlic is one of my favourites – so versatile and pungent, it appears for a short time from early April and can be found in shady woodlands (baby spinach is a perfect substitute here when wild garlic is not in season). Beautiful mussels, plump, sweet and salty, are particularly good in the months that contain the letter R – September to April – although they are available all year round).

SERVES 4

1 kg (2 lb 4 oz) live mussels, cleaned and debearded
3 tablespoons olive oil
6 rashers of smoked bacon, cut into lardons
200 ml (7 fl oz/scant 1 cup) Cornish cider
1 shallot, halved
1 bay leaf
1 small bunch of thyme
4 black peppercorns
30g (1 oz) unsalted butter
1 medium leek, trimmed and thinly sliced
227g (8 oz) clotted cream (I use Rodda's)
4 tablespoons chopped tarragon
4 tablespoons chopped flat-leaf parsley
150 g (5 oz) wild garlic or baby spinach
Cornish sea salt and freshly ground black pepper, to taste
wild garlic flowers, to garnish (optional)

TO SERVE

sourdough loaf or ciabatta, thickly sliced, for toasting
1 garlic clove, peeled

Make sure the mussels are well cleaned, running the shells under cold water. Discard any that are open.

Heat the oil in a large, deep pan that has a lid over a medium heat. Fry the bacon lardons until crispy, then remove with a slotted spoon and set aside.

Pour the cider into the pan, add the shallots, bay, thyme and peppercorns, and bring to a simmer. Tip in the mussels and cook, with the lid on, for 4–5 minutes, giving the pan a good shake to wake the mussels up and allow them to open. Remove the lid and tip the mussels into a colander set over a bowl to catch the delicious cider stock. Discard any mussels that remain closed.

Wipe out the pan and add the butter. When melted, add the leek and sauté gently until softened. Strain the cooking liquor and add to the pan, and cook until reduced by half. Add the clotted cream and simmer for 1–2 minutes, then add half of the cooked bacon lardons and and half of the tarragon and parsley. Stir gently and check for seasoning. Add the mussels back to the pan, along with the wild garlic or spinach and allow to wilt.

Meanwhile, toast some thick slices of bread and rub each one with a garlic clove.

Ladle the mussels into warm bowls or one big serving bowl. Finish off with the remaining bacon lardons, tarragon, parsley and wild garlic flowers (if using). Eat!

COOK'S NOTE This is so versatile, you can add whatever base ingredients you like. From classic *moules marinière* to fennel and lovage, or – a favourite – spaghetti with mussels and white beans. Makes a delicious starter or a bigger substantial lunch or supper. A great recipe for feeding a crowd. Always wash and debeard your mussels and discard any that are open at this stage; if they remain closed once cooked, discard.

Spaghetti Puttanesca

Spaghetti, tomatoes, black olives, capers and garlic (anchovies if you like) – all my favourite ingredients (hooray) in one pan. Simply delicious for two, you may have your *Lady and the Tramp* spaghetti-slurping moment. Also an easy dish to scale up to feed a crowd. Simply heat some olive oil in a saucepan, add tinned cherry tomatoes, garlic, capers, marjoram, dried red chilli and black olives and reduce. Toss in some cooked wholemeal spaghetti and serve with finely chopped marjoram or oregano (or just follow my recipe below).

SERVES 2 (GENEROUSLY)

- 250 g (9 oz) wholemeal spaghetti (or your preferred choice of pasta)
- 3 tablespoons olive oil, plus extra for drizzling
- 400 g (14 oz) tin of cherry tomatoes (or I often throw in a handful of fresh cherry tomatoes if I have them)
- 1 garlic clove, chopped
- 1½ tablespoons small capers, rinsed
- 16 black olives, stoned (pitted) and halved
- 1 small bunch of marjoram, leaves only
- 1½ teaspoons chilli (hot pepper) flakes
- 100 g (3½ oz) Parmesan, grated
- Cornish sea salt and freshly ground black pepper

Cook the spaghetti in a large saucepan of salted water for 10 minutes, or until al dente. Drain and reserve 100 ml (3½ fl oz/ scant ½ cup) of the pasta cooking water.

Meanwhile, place a frying pan (skillet) over a medium heat and add the olive oil. Stir in the tomatoes and garlic with a pinch of sea salt and cook over a high heat for 4–5 minutes, stirring often until reduced by half. Stir in the capers, black olives, most of the marjoram (reserve some leaves for garnish) and chilli flakes, and reduce for a further 2–3 minutes.

Add the cooked spaghetti to the sauce along with the reserved pasta cooking water and stir well until it all comes together. Divide the pasta puttanesca among pasta bowls and serve with extra olive oil, marjoram leaves and grated Parmesan.

COOK'S NOTES If fresh marjoram is unavailable, good-quality dried oregano or marjoram will work perfectly, or maybe a few basil leaves to garnish. Easy chilli that you can find in supermarkets is a great alternative to dried chilli, or just deseed and chop 1 fresh red chilli.

Kedgeree with Leeks, Spinach, Spring-Note Herbs, Crème Fraîche

Comfort in a bowl, there is something so nostalgic about kedgeree – or spicy rice, as we call it in our house. A dish that is so versatile, perfect for a weekend brunch or feeding a crowd, a moreish hangover cure, or a quick and simple midweek supper. Deliciously simple, it's also a great way to introduce children to cooking with fish. Salmon or haddock can replace the smoked fish, if you prefer.

SERVES 6

- 450 g (1 lb/2¼ cups) long-grain brown rice
- 200 ml (7 fl oz/scant 1 cup) milk
- 2 bay leaves
- 2 cardamom pods, split
- 650 g (1 lb 7 oz) undyed smoked haddock (from a sustainable source), pin boned
- 75 g (2½ oz) unsalted butter
- 1 tablespoon good olive oil
- 2 garlic cloves, finely chopped
- 3 leeks, trimmed and thinly sliced
- 1 teaspoon curry powder
- pinch of chilli (hot pepper) flakes
- 100 g (3½ oz) baby spinach, stalks removed, washed
- 1 x 200 g (7 oz) tub of crème fraîche
- 3 tablespoons flat-leaf parsley, roughly chopped
- 2 tablespoons coriander (cilantro), roughly chopped
- juice of 1 lemon
- 3 just hard-boiled eggs
- Cornish sea salt and freshly ground black pepper

Cook the rice in a pan of boiling water according to the packet instructions, then drain and refresh under cold water.

In a medium saucepan that has a lid, heat the milk with the bay leaves and cardamom pods. Bring to a simmer, then turn off the heat, add the haddock and let it gently poach in the milk for 10 minutes covered with the lid. Carefully remove the fish to a plate with a slotted spoon and remove any skin or bones. Reserve the milk. Set both aside.

Heat the butter and olive oil in a large frying pan (skillet) over a medium heat, add the garlic and leeks and gently cook for 10–15 minutes. Never rush anything from the allium family. Stir in the curry powder and chilli flakes and gently cook out the spices. Gently fold in the rice so it stays light and fluffy, then stir in the warm milk and bring back to a simmer. Stir in the spinach leaves and cook for 3–5 minutes until just wilted. Stir in the crème fraîche, season with sea salt and black pepper, then stir in most of the chopped herbs and the lemon juice. Fork in the poached fish. Taste and consider. Halve the eggs lengthways and arrange on top with the remaining herbs.

You can serve in warm serving bowls, but I love nothing more than serving this from the pan placed in the middle of the table for everyone to share.

COOK'S NOTE A sprinkling of piment d'espelette (Basque-style mild red pepper) will add a little kick.

Sunshine Saffron Risotto

Cause a stir with this delicious recipe. I have written about my love for saffron on page 162 and this recipe is one of my favourites. Quick and simple and so versatile, when you have mastered risotto it will become your go-to recipe. Just a few ingredients that bring so much pleasure.

SERVES 4

1 teaspoon saffron
juice of ½ lemon
1 tablespoon good olive oil
50 g (2 oz) unsalted butter
2 shallots, finely chopped
350 g (12 oz/genrous 1½ cups) Carnaroli rice
200 ml (7 fl oz/scant 1 cup) white wine
800 ml (27 fl oz/generous 3¼ cups) chicken stock, warm
100 g (3½ oz) Parmesan, finely grated
4 tablespoons roughly chopped flat-leaf parsley

Place the saffron in a small bowl, squeeze over the lemon juice and leave to steep for a few minutes.

Heat the olive oil and half of the butter in a large saucepan over a medium heat. Add the shallots and cook until softened and translucent, then add the saffron mixture and stir in the rice. Stir for 1 minute, then pour in the wine and stir until almost absorbed. Add the warm chicken stock, ladleful by ladleful, and keep stirring for 20 minutes until the rice is cooked al dente (you may have some stock remaining).

Stir in the remaining butter and three-quarters of the Parmesan. Check for seasoning.

Ladle into warm bowls and serve sprinkled with the remaining Parmesan and the chopped parsley.

COOK'S NOTE Arborio rice is a good replacement for Carnaroli rice. A soft poached egg served on top is another delicious addition.

Blackberry & Peach Crisp

Give me pudding every day. I love fruit crumbles and pies and there is nothing better than making a sweet treat for the people you love. This recipe is so simple and versatile. I use it to top fruit throughout the seasons. It is lighter than a traditional oat crumble topping, and delicious served with custard or crème fraîche.

SERVES 4

FOR THE AMARETTI CRUMBLE TOPPING

160 g (5½ oz) amaretti biscuits
80 g (3 oz/scant 1 cup) flaked (slivered) almonds
75 g (2½ oz) unsalted butter, at room temperature
50 g (2 oz/scant ½ cup) plain (all-purpose) flour
50 g (2 oz/scant ¼ cup) caster (superfine) sugar

FOR THE BRAMBLE AND PEACH FILLING

350 g (12 oz) blackberries
6 peaches, skinned and stoned (pitted), sliced (if using frozen peaches, thaw and drain first)
100 g (3½ oz/scant ½ cup) caster (superfine) sugar
3 tablespoons cornflour (cornstarch) slaked with 2 tablespoons water
zest and juice of ½ lemon

Preheat the oven to 200°C (180°C fan/400°F/Gas 6).

For the crumble topping, blitz the amaretti biscuits with the flaked almonds in a food processor to a rubble.

In a mixing bowl, rub the butter and flour together to resemble breadcrumbs, then add the sugar along with the almond rubble and mix together.

Spread the mixture out over a baking sheet and bake in the oven for 10–15 minutes until golden. Allow to cool.

For the filling, place the blackberries, peaches, sugar, cornflour mixture and lemon zest and juice in a heavy-based saucepan and slowly bring to a simmer, stirring all the time to allow the sugar to dissolve. Cook until the fruit is tender. Transfer to an oven-to-table baking dish and sprinkle over the amaretti crumble topping. Finish off in the oven for 5–6 minutes.

Don't forget the cream.

COOK'S NOTE Perfect topping for poached vanilla apricots, plums and apples, blackberries, pears or candy-pink rhubarb and cardamom. This recipe also works beautifully cooked over fire, cooking the fruit in a heatproof dish and then adding the topping.

Creamy Rice Pudding with Cardamom & Coconut

This is a simple rice pudding made with coconut milk, double (heavy) cream, clotted cream, cardamom and vanilla, served with dollops of my Strawberry and Elderflower Jam (see page 230). To be honest, old-school rice pudding was always my food hell, but the coconut and citrussy, piney, fruity notes of cardamom here completely transfrom it from my childhood experience. Creamy and fragrant – and nothing like that rice pudding from the ’80s – this pudding has won my heart and my family love it.

SERVES 4

- 1 tablespoon coconut oil
- 150 g (5 oz/generous ⅔ cup) pudding rice
- 450 ml (15 fl oz/1¾ cups) coconut milk
- 250 ml (8½ fl oz/1 cup) double (heavy) cream
- 50 g (2 oz/¼ cup) golden caster (superfine) sugar
- 2 cardamom pods, lightly crushed with the back of a knife
- 1 vanilla pod, split lengthways
- 200 g (7 oz/scant 1 cup) clotted cream
- elderflowers, when in season, to decorate (optional)

Heat the coconut oil in a heavy-based saucepan over a low-medium heat. Once melted, add the rice and stir to coat, then cook for 1 minute. Pour in the coconut milk and double cream, then stir in the sugar, cardamom and vanilla pods. Bring to the boil, then reduce the heat and simmer for 15 minutes. Keep stirring until the rice grains are tender and plump and the liquid has reduced by around half.

When cooked, stir in the clotted cream and remove the cardamom and vanilla pods.

Serve warm with dollops of strawberry jam (or any jam that takes your fancy). Or leave to cool completely, chill in the refrigerator and serve cold, decorated with elderflowers, when in season, if wished.

COOK’S NOTE It’s all in the stir – keep the rice moving and be patient. If you have extra double cream, serve a dollop on the top.

CHATEAU

Crème Brûlée with Vanilla

I often have a craving for crème brûlée – set custard, vanillary, cool and creamy with a delicate sugary crust. I have experimented with my recipe over the years, using crème fraîche, double (heavy) cream, or half and half, but now I find a combination of double cream and milk gives the lightest of textures. A split vanilla pod is essential and I use icing (confectioner's) sugar for the caramel.

SERVES 6

- 50 ml (1¾ fl oz/3 tablespoons) whole milk
- 450 ml (15 fl oz/1¾ cups) double (heavy) cream
- 1 vanilla pod, split
- 5 medium free-range egg yolks
- 80 g (3 oz/⅓ cup) golden caster (superfine) sugar
- 50 g (2 oz/scant ½ cup) icing (confectioner's) sugar

FRUIT (OPTIONAL) PER RAMEKIN

- a couple of raspberries
- 1 teaspoon blackcurrants
- 1 teaspoon passion fruit

Preheat the oven to 170°C (150°C fan/340°F/Gas 3).

To make the custard, place the milk and cream in a small pan and scrape the seeds from the vanilla pod into the mixture. Add the whole pod to the pan, too, and bring to a simmer, then turn off the heat and leave to infuse for at least 15 minutes.

Meanwhile, beat the egg yolks and caster sugar together in a large mixing bowl.

Remove the vanilla pod from the cream mixture and pour it over the egg yolk mixture, whisking all the time to combine.

Divide the custard among 6 ramekins, then place them in a deep roasting tray. Place the tray in the oven and carefully pour in enough warm water to reach halfway up sides of the ramekins. Bake for 30 minutes, or until the custard is just set.

Leave to cool and then refrigerate. (I love the texture of cold custard against the warm sugar crust, but if you prefer you can leave the brûlée at room temperature at this stage.)

When ready to serve, sprinkle a thin layer of the icing sugar on top of each ramekin and place them under a hot grill (broiler) until golden brown. Alternatively, use a kitchen blowtorch to caramelise the tops.

COOK'S NOTE Fruit is completely optional, but I love the surprise of finding a pop of colour and tartness hidden under the creamy set custard. You can keep the egg whites to make my baby meringues on page 78, or they freeze well – I always use an ice-cube tray for this and then you can pop them out when you need them.

the

On

(AHOY THERE)

Boat

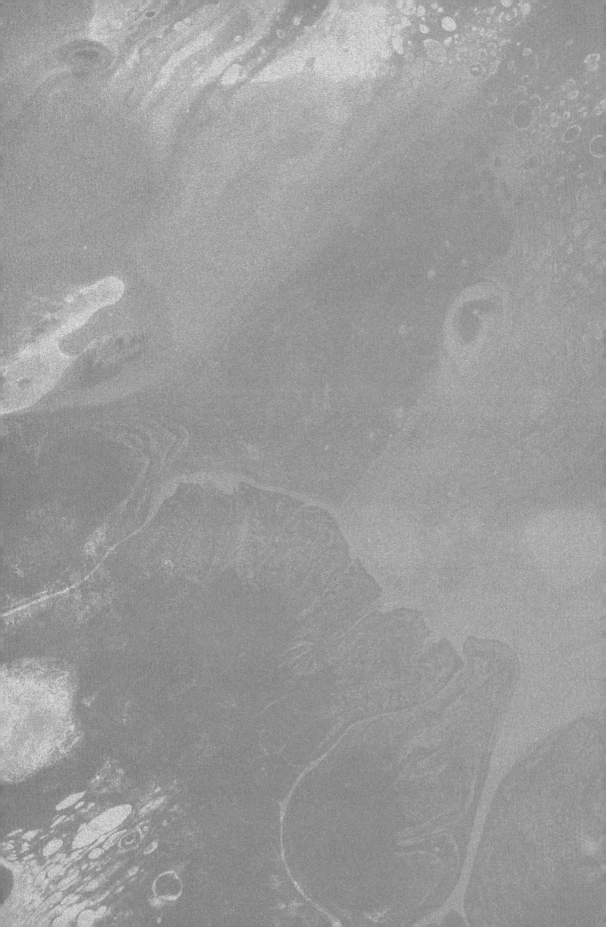

BOTTLE blue. Fair winds, chasing colours and away you go. Living in Cornwall there is always a boat involved, whether it is a dingy, kayak, tender, fishing boat or one with sails, it is hard not to be wooed by the open seas or gentler rivers of the south coast. Rolling on the sea or messing about on boats is such a wonderful way of seeing the beautiful Cornish coastline – there is something magical about looking at the land from the sea. Whether you are sailing up the Helford River, along the soft, almost tropical, south coast, or rolling around on the open northern seas luring in mackerel, there is nothing better than the salty sea air. As always the Cornish weather is unpredictable, so a bag packed with food, just in case, is always sensible. Boat food needs to be easy and practical: a flask of soup, a crab sandwich, focaccia and hummus.

Cantaloupe Gazpacho

This is for my Dadio, who has always loved gazpacho and has always loved boats, whether sailing on the south coast, the faster waters of the estuary at Rock, or beyond the lands of Cornwall. It's a perfect lunch for messing about on boats, or on the beach or in the garden. Colour, colour, colour – a beautiful soup or gentle curry for the warmer days of the year.

SERVES 4

1 kg (2 lb 4 oz) ripe cantaloupe melon
2 tablespoons olive oil
4 shallots, chopped
8 lemongrass stalks, tough outer leaves removed, thinly sliced
1 green chilli, finely sliced
1 tablespoon chopped fresh root ginger
zest and juice of 1 orange
4 kaffir (makrut) lime leaves
400 g (14 oz) can of coconut milk
zest and juice of 3 limes, or more as needed
1 small bunch of coriander (cilantro), chopped
1 small bunch of mint, leaves only, chopped
Cornish sea salt and freshly ground black pepper

TO GARNISH

chopped fresh herbs, such as mint, coriander (cilantro) and basil
edible flowers
olive oil, for drizzling
lime wedges

Halve the melon, scoop out and discard the seeds and chop the flesh into chunks. Set aside.

Heat 1 tablespoon of the olive oil in a saucepan over a medium heat, add the shallots, lemongrass, chilli, ginger, orange zest and juice, and a pinch of salt, and sauté, stirring, until the shallots are translucent. Do this as gently as possible as you do not want any colour. Add the lime leaves and melon (if you plan to serve it in bowls later, keep 8 small chunks of melon back for garnish), and season once again with a little salt. Reduce the heat to very low and simmer very gently, stirring occasionally, until the melon has completely fallen apart. This could take up to about 30 minutes.

Remove from the heat, stir in the coconut milk, lime zest and juice and leave to cool.

Once cool, remove the lime leaves and blend the soup in a food processor until smooth. Pass through a sieve (fine mesh strainer) for a really smooth texture. Taste and season with more salt and pepper and lime juice, if needed. Refrigerate until chilled.

Serve in bowls or mugs with the reserved melon pieces (if using), chopped herbs and edible flowers, a drizzle of olive oil and extra lime wedges.

COOK'S NOTE Cantaloupe melon is essential to get the bright orange colour. Kaffir lime leaves keep well in the freezer.

Carrot & Miso Hummus with Parsley & Coriander

This hummus is so simple to make and loved by all – children and adults alike. We use miso so much at my restaurant and it is becoming an ingredient that is widely available. This is a great recipe to try if you have never used it before. Moreish with umami flavour.

SERVES 4

- 1 kg (2 lb 4 oz) carrots, peeled
- 2 tablespoons olive oil (I use Fowey Valley olive oil), plus extra to serve
- 100 g (3½ oz/generous ⅓ cup) plain yoghurt
- juice of 1 lemon
- 2 teaspoons white miso paste
- Cornish sea salt and freshly ground black pepper

TO SERVE

- 1 tablespoon chopped coriander (cilantro)
- 1 tablespoon chopped flat-leaf parsley

Preheat the oven to 200°C (180°C fan/400°F/Gas 6).

Place the carrots whole in a roasting tray, drizzle with the olive oil and sprinkle with sea salt. Roast for 45 minutes–1 hour until golden and sweet. Be patient here – the longer the carrots are given, the sweeter they become. Remove from the oven and leave to cool.

When cool, crush the carrots with the back of a fork and then place them in a food processor along with the yoghurt, lemon juice and miso. Blitz, adding up to 250 ml (8½ fl oz/1 cup) water to let it down to your desired consistency, then taste and check the seasoning.

To serve, drizzle with some more olive oil and top with the chopped coriander and parsley.

COOK'S NOTE If you are like me, I sometimes need something to eat in between lunch and supper. Instead of reaching for something sweet, this is always a good thing with crackers or a piece of toast.

Rosemary & Sea Salt Focaccia

Daily bread and breadmaking is so good for the soul. Focaccia is very forgiving, so it's always my go-to bread. Allow to cool and then serve in slices or toast.

SERVES 8–12

500 g (1 lb 2 oz/4 cups) strong white (bread) flour
20 g (¾ oz) fresh yeast (or 7 g/¼ oz fast action dried yeast)
1½ teaspoons granulated sugar
1½ teaspoons fine table salt
360 ml (11½ fl oz/scant 1½ cups) tepid water
15 g (½ oz/2 tablespoons) fine semolina
25 ml (1 fl oz/1½ tablespoons) good olive oil, plus extra for drizzling
a small handful of fresh rosemary sprigs
Cornish sea salt flakes, for sprinkling

Place the flour in the bowl of a stand mixer fitted with the dough hook attachment. Crumble in the yeast on one side of the bowl, along with the sugar, and add the salt to the other side of the bowl. Start the machine on slow and begin to incorporate the water. Once all the water has been added, set the machine on medium speed and leave to knead for 8–10 minutes.

Meanwhile, line a shallow baking tin (pan), 25 x 34 cm (10 x 14 in) with baking parchment and dust with the semolina. Once kneaded, place the dough in the tray, cover with the oil and spread out the dough to fill the tray. Cover with cling film (plastic wrap) and leave to prove in a warm place for 1 hour, or until doubled in size.

Remove the cling film, drizzle the dough with more olive oil, cover again and leave to prove for a further 30 minutes.

Sprinkle the focaccia with sea salt and make holes with your thumb across the dough and spike with the tops of the rosemary sprigs, then drizzle with more oil.

Meanwhile, preheat the oven to 240°C (220°C fan/475°F/Gas 9).

Bake the foccacia for 20–25 minutes until golden brown.

Turn out onto a cooling rack, drizzle with more olive oil, sprinkle with extra sea salt and rosemary leaves, then leave to cool.

COOK'S NOTE You can top focaccia with olives, sunblush tomatoes, sea herbs, thyme and so on. Fresh and dried yeast are interchangeable in recipes, but remember that you need to use twice as much fresh yeast (by weight) than dried. For this, I usually use a baking pan from my bake set by Falcon Enamelware.

Radish, Unsalted Butter, Cornish Sea Salt

I often talk about simplicity and, as many of you know, I have been banging the simplicity drum for a while now. This recipe – or three components – is a perfect example of this. Use quality ingredients and think about presentation. This is one of my favourite ways to eat radishes. In my restaurant, we often serve them like this or with whipped cod's roe. Make sure the butter is well softened so the radish effortlessly picks it up.

SERVES 2

- 125 g (4 oz) unsalted butter, softened
- 2 tablespoons milk
- 1 bunch of radishes with leaves, washed
- 4 tablespoons Cornish sea salt

Place the softened butter in a bowl, add the milk and beat for 5–6 minutes until pale and creamy.

Cut some of the radishes in half and leave some whole, then divide them between two small plates. Spoon some softened butter onto each plate and sprinkle a pile of sea salt next to it. The idea is to dip the radishes in the butter and then the salt. For a slightly smarter version, rocher the butter (see note).

COOK'S NOTE A rocher is an oval shape of butter, ice cream, sorbet, paté, etc. made with one spoon, whereas a quenelle is formed using two spoons. A rocher of butter looks so pretty and is well worth learning to do. A good way to learn is to buy a tub of ice cream and practice using a spoon dipped in some hot water. There are lots of videos online explaining the technique. Practice makes perfect.

Cornish Crab Sandwich

Cold box at the ready. Good brown bread, fresh Cornish crab, mayo, lemon juice, sea salt, black pepper and a handful of rocket (arugula). I am immediately transported to Port Isaac, sitting on a bench on the platt looking out through the harbour wall to the open sea. All the scents of the sea, lobster and crab pots stacked high, waiting to be taken on board ship to catch the rich pickings from the ocean beyond. Seagulls overhead making the most noise as usual, the working harbour, the fishermen coming in and out depending on the tide. I think a crab sandwich should be kept simple – let the freshly picked Cornish crab do the talking. No brown meat for me, simply white crab meat with mayonnaise to bring it together.

MAKES 2

- 100 g (3½ oz) Cornish white crab meat
- 2 tablespoons mayonnaise
- 4 slices of granary loaf
- salted butter, softened
- a handful of rocket (arugula) leaves or round lettuce leaves
- juice of 1 lemon
- Cornish sea salt and freshly ground black pepper

Check for any shell by placing the crab meat on a tray and gently sorting through the meat with your hands (gloves are good for this task) from one end to the other.

Place the picked crab meat and mayonnaise in a bowl, add a pinch of sea salt and grind or two of black pepper, and mix together. Butter the bread and add the rocket or lettuce, then spoon on the crab mixture. Add a squeeze of lemon and sandwich together.

COOK'S NOTE Do not compromise on ingredients here, always seek the best quality crab meat. For me, Just Shellfish in Port Isaac is always the place to find this.

Salad Niçoise

All the good things in one salad – that salad from the south of France. No introduction is needed really. Niçoise is a salad that is in no way shy – salty, fresh and full of flavour, it makes a substantial lunch or supper on its own. Anchovies are optional, but really a Niçoise would be lost without them. Quail eggs if you prefer smaller egg action and I have added mangetout (snow peas) just for some extra green crunch.

SERVES 4

- 4 medium free-range eggs
- 100 g (3½ oz) French beans
- 100 g (3½ oz) mangetout (snow peas)
- 2 little gem lettuce
- 200 g (7 oz) cherry tomatoes, at room temperature
- 6 anchovy fillets, drained and rinsed (optional)
- 2 tablespoons capers
- 16 black olives, stoned (pitted) and halved
- 1 small bunch of flat-leaf parsley, chopped
- 1 small bunch of chervil, chopped

FOR THE DRESSING

- juice of 2 lemons
- 1 teaspoon Dijon mustard
- 2 teaspoons runny honey
- 6 tablespoons good olive oil
- Cornish sea salt and freshly ground black pepper

Place the eggs in a pan of water, bring to the boil and cook for 5–6 minutes until just hard-boiled. Remove to a bowl of cold water to stop them cooking.

Bring another pan of water to the boil, add the French beans and mangetout and blanch, then refresh in ice-cold water to keep their colour.

For the dressing, whisk together the lemon juice, mustard and honey with a good pinch of sea salt and some freshly ground black pepper. Drizzle in the olive oil slowly, whisking until the dressing emulsifies. Taste and add more oil if it's too citrussy.

Wash the lettuce and pat dry, then tear off the leaves from the stalk and arrange them in a shallow salad bowl. Cut the tomatoes in half and mix in with the leaves, then add the anchovies (if using), capers and olives. Drain the French beans and mangetout, pat dry and add to the salad. Add the dressing and toss together.

Cut the eggs into quarters or halves and arrange on top of the salad, then scatter with the parsley and chervil and season with more salt and pepper.

COOK'S NOTES I find adding all the dressing ingredients to a jam jar with a tight-fitting lid and shaking together is a great way to make dressings. Broad beans, artichoke hearts and broccoli are delicious alternative greens. Whatever you do, this salad wants to be seen.

Caraway-Seeded Sausages Rolls with Apricots & Honey

Sausage rolls are one of life's joys. Eat them warm straight from the oven or cold on a picnic, wrapped in parchment paper and tucked into a tin for the perfect boat-time crib (see page 65).

MAKES 8

500 g (1 lb 2 oz) free-range sausagemeat or minced (ground) pork
100 g (3½ oz) dried apricots, roughly chopped
50 g (2 oz/scant ⅔ cup) fresh breadcrumbs
2 tablespoons milk
1½ tablespoons wholegrain mustard
5 sprigs of thyme, leaves only
1 large free-range egg, beaten
500 g (1 lb 2 oz) packet of readymade puff pastry, halved
plain (all-purpose) flour, for dusting
2 teaspoons caraway seeds
3 tablespoons clear honey

Line a large baking sheet with baking parchment.

In a large bowl, mix together the sausagemeat, apricots, breadcrumbs, milk, mustard, thyme and half of the egg until combined.

Roll out each pastry half on a lightly floured surface to a thickness of about 5 mm (¼ in) to form two 35 x 20 cm (14 x 8 in) rectangles. Divide the filling mixture in half and arrange each portion along the long edge of each pastry rectangle, shaping each into a sausage shape, ensuring they reach from end to end. Brush the other long edge with the remaining beaten egg and tightly roll up the pastry to enclose the filling. Press lightly to seal the join, then trim and crimp. Cut each roll into 5 cm (2 in) rolls and arrange on the prepared baking sheet. Sprinkle with the caraway seeds. Chill in the refrigerator for 20 minutes.

Meanwhile, preheat the oven to 220°C (200°C fan/ 430°F/Gas 8).

Bake for 25–30 minutes until golden brown.

Warm the honey in a pan over a medium heat and brush each sausage roll with the runny glaze. Leave to rest for at least 10 minutes.

COOK'S NOTE Perfect crib time snack (see page 65) or the all-time best party food. Short, flaky or puff? Always puff pastry for me, buttery delicious layers of goodness. Switch up the filling with apples, sage and fennel seeds, spice it up or make it a festive canapé. A great recipe to bake with children as it introduces them to rolling pastry and they are such fun to make throughout the year.

Summer Coleslaw

Homemade coleslaw or cabbage salad is a thing of beauty (unlike the store-bought version). Pointed cabbage, carrots, kohlrabi, Pink Lady apples, fennel (fronds and all), all thinly sliced with generous handfuls of parsley and coriander (cilantro), a splash of good vinegar, a squeeze of lemon, some Cornish sea salt and a big dollop or two of crème fraîche – deeeelicious and even better the next day!

SERVES 6

¼ medium pointed cabbage, finely shredded
¼ red cabbage, finely shredded
2 fennel bulbs, finely shredded
4 carrots, peeled and grated
1 kohlrabi, finely shredded
2 Pink Lady apples, washed, cored and thinly sliced
1 bunch of radishes, washed and thinly sliced
zest and juice of 1 lemon
1 tablespoon Dijon mustard
50 ml (1¾ fl oz/3 tablespoons) cider vinegar
200 g (7 oz/generous ¾ cup) crème fraîche
1 small bunch of flat-leaf parsley, finely chopped
1 small bunch of coriander (cilantro), finely chopped
Cornish sea salt and freshly ground black pepper

Prepare all the vegetables and place in a large bowl, season with salt and pepper, the lemon zest and juice, mustard and cider vinegar, then bring it all together with the crème fraîche and the chopped herbs. Taste and consider all the flavours.

COOK'S NOTE A food processor is a really great gadget to invest in and perfect for making coleslaw. I love the process of slicing and shredding, but if you are short on time a processor is a wonderful thing. Mayonnaise can be substituted for the crème fraîche.

Cornish Charcuterie, Caperberries

This is not a recipe as such, but always a great small plate to share. For me, keep whatever charcuterie you choose very thinly sliced. Caperberries are a key ingredient here, bringing acidity and piquancy.

SERVES AS MANY AS YOU LIKE

fennel salami (my favourite)
salami Napoli
coppa ham
bresaola
a handful of caperberries
good olive oil, for drizzling
sourdough bread, for slicing
Preserved Summer Tomatoes (see page 238), to serve

Arrange the charcuterie attractively on a plate, top with caperberries and a drizzle of good olive oil. Serve with slices of sourdough and maybe some preserved tomatoes.

COOK'S NOTE Duchy Charcuterie has been quietly and consistently making delicious charcuterie in North Cornwall and you need to know about it.

Gorse-Flower Fudge

Life is sweet. The windy open cliffs covered in bright yellow gorse are very much part of the beautiful wild landscape of Cornwall. Sea pinks appear on the coast framing the cliff edges, and the seaside hedgerows never disappoint. Gorse has delicious coconut-scented flowers that lend a beautiful perfume to this fudge. Soft and crumbly, this is the sweetest treat.

SERVES 10

- 300 g (10½ oz) unsalted butter, plus extra melted for greasing the tin
- 45 g (1¾ oz/2 tablespoons) golden syrup
- 900 g (2 lb/scant 4 cups) caster (superfine) sugar
- 150 ml (5 fl oz/scant ⅔ cup) of the thick part of a tin of coconut milk
- 150 ml (5 fl oz/scant ⅔ cup) double (heavy) cream
- a good handful of gorse flowers
- a sprinkling of dessicated (dried shredded) coconut

Gently melt the butter, syrup, sugar, coconut milk and cream in a heavy-based pan, then bring the mixture to a rolling boil. When it reaches 115°C (239°F) on a sugar thermometer, turn off the heat and leave for 10 minutes.

Meanwhile, line a 23 cm (9 in) square baking tin (pan) with foil and lightly grease with melted butter.

Stir a good handful of gorse flower petals into the fudge mixture and stir until it begins to thicken and come away from the bottom of the pan. Pour into the lined tin and sprinkle with coconut and more gorse petals. Set in the refrigerator for 3 hours or overnight.

Once set, you can use the foil to lift the fudge from the tin. Cut into squares.

COOK'S NOTE Be careful when picking gorse – it is gnarly and the stalks are prickly, but the flowers make up for this initial unfriendliness. If you have not eaten all the fudge and need to store it, place a sheet of greaseproof (wax) paper between the layers to keep them from sticking together. Fudge will keep for 3 weeks in an airtight container in a cool place or in the refrigerator.

Rum Chocolate Brownies with Bourbon Biscuits

Ahoy there me hearties. Cornish spiced rum seems only appropriate in these dark chocolate and rum squares, perfect to keep your sugar levels up. I am obsessed with Bourbon biscuits, always breaking them in half and eating the insides first. Here, they sit perfectly on top of the rum brownie and always get eaten with excitement.

MAKES 16

- 180 g (6½ oz) salted butter
- 160 g (5½ oz) dark chocolate
- 3 medium free-range eggs
- 300 g (10½ oz/1⅓ cups) golden caster (superfine) sugar
- 80 g (3 oz/scant ⅔ cup) plain (all-purpose) flour
- 45 g (1¾ oz/generous ⅓ cup) cocoa powder
- 1 tablespoon Cornish spiced rum (or any good rum)
- 1 pack of Bourbon biscuits

Line a 20 cm (8 in) square baking tin (pan) with baking parchment.

Melt the butter and chocolate in a heatproof bowl set over a pan of gently simmering water. Allow to cool.

In a separate bowl, beat the eggs and sugar until thickened and pale. Pour in the cooled chocolate mixture, then sift over the flour and cocoa powder. Gently fold the mixture together, then add the rum and fold that in too.

Pour the batter into the prepared tin and top with the Bourbon biscuits. Bake in the oven for 20–25 minutes until just set.

COOK'S NOTES Use decent dark chocolate, at least 54% but ideally 70% cocoa solids. Most good supermarkets stock this. Custard creams are equally as good as Bourbon biscuits.

BOURBON
BOURBON
BOURBON
BOURBON
BOURBON
BOURBON

Soirées

Seaside

(AT THE END OF THE DAY)

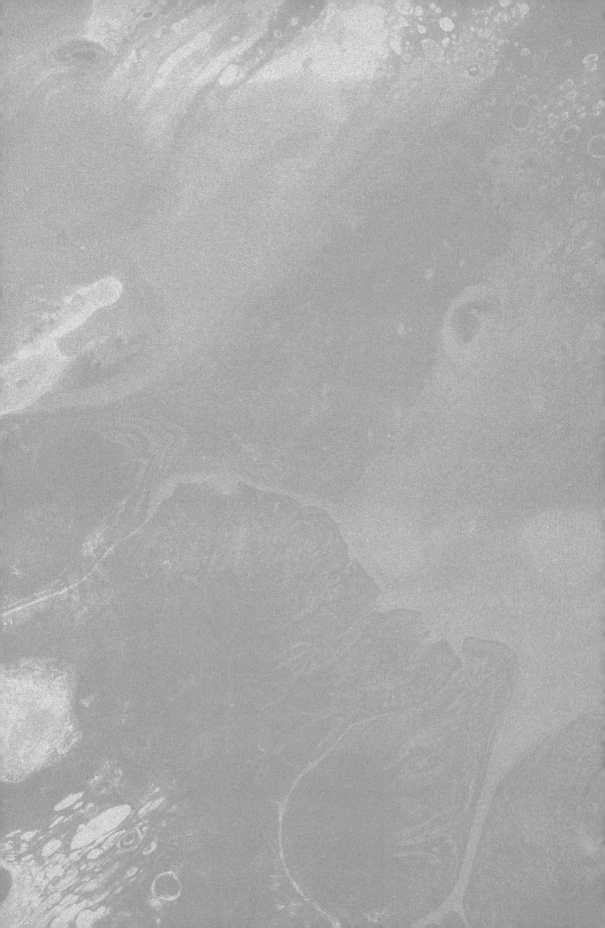

FADED ticking greens and blues. Fish supper cravings. Nothing says coastal life more to me than eating seafood cooked over coals by the sea. Salty air, the sound of the waves rolling in and out, the breeze lifting my spirits and bringing a sense of well-being and happiness. Our house at Harlyn is framed by tamarisk trees and a pathway that leads from the garden over the stile, and through the well-kept fields to the beach. We often eat outside underneath the ash tree, weather permitting, and more often than not we head to the beach and build a firepit to cook over coals. In true bracing British style, we do this on colder days, too. The recipes in this chapter can be oven-baked, cooked on a barbecue, or on a firepit built into the sand (always get permission before you build a firepit on the beach, ensure it is extinguished responsibly and take your rubbish home). The excitement of planning what we are going to eat always takes up our time, our hunger for the next meal after a day on the water or exploring the land is always such a highlight for us.

Cornish Scallops, Beurre Blanc, Chives, Fennel

Simple seafood joys. Colour on a grey day. Warmth and comfort. This is one of my favourite recipes – I love the classics and this beautiful scallop starter in a butter sauce (*beurre blanc*) celebrates my affinity with France and, of course, the Cornish seaside. And fennel is so versatile – delicious raw or cooked. A dish that will dazzle, with minimal preparation and cooking, it's a perfect classy starter for supper with friends, bringing a coastal feel to your table.

SERVES 4 (ALLOWING 3 SCALLOPS EACH)

12 scallops (roe on, roe off, entirely up to you – personally, I prefer no roe)
sunflower oil, for brushing
juice of 1 lemon
1 fennel bulb, fronds and all, finely sliced
2 shallots, finely chopped
75 ml (2½ fl oz/5 tablespoons) dry white wine vinegar
75 ml (2½ fl oz/ 5 tablespoons) white wine
75 ml (2½ fl oz/ 5 tablespoons) water
150 g (5 oz) cold unsalted butter, cut into cubes
1 teaspoon finely chopped chives
a splash of Pernod, if you are feeling over-excited
Cornish sea salt and white pepper

Prepare the scallops: pull off the pale white frill and any other pieces around the scallop to leave you with a sweet, plump, clean-looking scallop (or ask your fishmonger).

Place the scallops on a plate, brush with sunflower oil, season lightly with sea salt and set aside.

Squeeze the lemon juice into a bowl, add the finely sliced fennel and feathery fronds and toss in the juice. Set aside.

Place the shallots, vinegar and white wine in a pan along with the water. Bring to a gentle simmer and reduce until almost all the liquid has gone. Reduce the heat to very low and whisk in the cubes of cold butter, one piece at a time. Once all the butter has been added, the sauce should resemble a thin custard. Remove from the heat and set aside. Add the chopped chives and taste for seasoning.

Heat a heavy-based frying pan and pan-fry the scallops for 2 minutes until they are caramelised in colour, then turn and cook for another minute. Time to add that splash of Pernod, if you are feeling it.

Divide the butter sauce among warm serving plates. Place 3 scallops on each plate and garnish each scallop with fine shards of fennel. Eat with happiness and mop up any butter left on the plate with some bread.

COOK'S NOTE A quick supper that I sometimes make for my family: use *beurre blanc* to finish off spaghetti with chilli and sage.

Roasted Asparagus, Hazelnuts, Garlic, Marjoram, Sourdough Crumbs

One of my favourite ways to cook these gorgeous green spears is gently roasted with good olive oil, sea salt and black pepper, then simply served with a delicious nutty, herby sourdough crumb. Alternatively, lie the asparagus on a bed of crème fraîche sauce (see my Cook's note) for added richness.

SERVES 4–6

- 50 g (2 oz/generous ⅓ cup) hazelnuts, skin on
- 100 ml (3½ fl oz/scant ½ cup) good olive oil, plus a drizzle for the asparagus
- 150 g (5 oz/scant 2 cups) fresh sourdough breadcrumbs
- 1 bunch of fresh marjoram or oregano, leaves only
- 2 garlic cloves, crushed
- 600 g (1 lb 5 oz) asparagus
- zest and juice of 1 lemon
- Cornish sea salt and freshly ground black pepper
- edible flowers (borage, violas, primroses), to garnish

Preheat the oven to 200°C (180°C fan/400°F/Gas 6).

Place the hazelnuts on a baking sheet and roast for 6–8 minutes in the middle of the oven until lightly roasted. Remove from the oven, wrap the hazelnuts in a clean dish towel, then rub them to remove the skins (don't worry about any skins that don't come off – they add texture and colour). Allow to cool, then crush roughly with a pestle and mortar or the end of a rolling pin. Set aside.

Heat half of the olive oil in a large frying pan (skillet) over a medium heat. Add the breadcrumbs, most of the marjoram or oregano, garlic and a pinch of sea salt, and cook for 4–5 minutes, or until lightly golden. Set aside.

Wash and trim off the hard ends from the asparagus, then arrange the spears on a baking sheet lined with baking parchment. Drizzle with a little olive oil and season with sea salt and freshly ground black pepper. Bake for 10 minutes, or until the spears are lightly browned and tender.

Arrange the asparagus on a large serving platter and sprinkle over the crushed hazelnuts, sourdough crumbs, lemon zest and remaining marjoram or oregano.

Place the lemon juice and remaining olive oil in a small bowl, with a pinch each of salt and pepper, whisk to combine, then drizzle over the asparagus. Finish with edible flowers and serve.

COOK'S NOTE Warm 100 g (3½ oz/generous ⅓ cup) crème fraîche in a pan and gently stir in 50 g (2 oz) finely grated Parmesan. Spoon onto plates and sit the roasted asparagus on top.

Helford Blue, Spring Onion, Leek, Crème Fraîche & Thyme Tart

Shortcrust pastry, blue cheese, sweet leeks, free-range eggs, mascarpone and herbs. Soft, pale and delicious Helford blue cheese is one of my favourites. I always have it on my cheese board and its creamy texture works beautifully with the alliums here.

SERVES 8

FOR THE SHORTCRUST PASTRY
- 250 g (9 oz/2 cups) plain (all-purpose) flour, plus extra for dusting
- 100 g (3½ oz) unsalted butter
- a pinch of Cornish sea salt
- 2 medium free-range egg yolks
- 2–3 tablespoons milk

FOR THE FILLING
- 50 g (2 oz) unsalted butter
- 225 g (8 oz) leeks, trimmed, washed and sliced (discard any tough outer layers)
- 4 spring onions (scallions), trimmed and sliced
- 2 tablespoons thyme leaves, plus extra to garnish
- 100 g (3½ oz/generous ⅓ cup) crème fraîche
- 100 ml (3½ fl oz/scant ½ cup) double (heavy) cream
- 2 medium free-range eggs, plus 1 egg yolk
- 150 g (5 oz) Helford blue cheese (or similar)
- Cornish sea salt and freshly ground black pepper

To make the pastry, combine the flour, butter, sea salt and egg yolks in a food processor and pulse. Once combined, let it down with a little milk until it all comes together as a dough. Cover with cling film (plastic wrap) and leave it to rest in the refrigerator for at least 2 hours.

On a lightly floured work surface, roll out the pastry to 1 cm (½ in) thick and use it to line a 22 cm (9 in) fluted loose-bottomed tart tin (pan). Chill for 30 minutes.

Meanwhile, preheat the oven to 200°C (180°C fan/400°F/Gas 6).

Blind bake the pastry case for 20–25 minutes, then trim off any excess pastry.

For the filling, melt the butter in a frying pan (skillet) over a medium heat, add the leeks, spring onions and thyme, and gently cook for 8–10 minutes until softened.

Whisk the crème fraîche, cream, eggs and egg yolk together in a bowl and season with salt and pepper.

Arrange the leek and spring onion mixture over the base of the tart, crumble the Helford blue on top, then pour over the cream mixture.

Bake the tart for 25–30 minutes until golden and firm in the centre. Leave to rest for 10 minutes before slicing and serve with extra thyme leaves on top.

COOK'S NOTES The pastry freezes well raw or even when blind baked. Swap out the leeks for slowly caramelised red onions and the blue cheese for goats' cheese. Always cook alliums slowly, as this brings out their natural sweetness.

Whole Mackerel Over Coals with Garlic & Garden Leaves

For me, cooking these little fish over coals to blacken the skin is the perfect way to eat them. I have spent many hours mackerel fishing off the coast of Cornwall – they will always have a place at my table, especially when cooked over coals.

SERVES 6

- 6 tablespoons good olive oil
- zest of 1 lemon
- 3 garlic cloves, crushed
- 1½ teaspoons chilli (hot pepper) flakes
- 2 tablespoons chopped flat-leaf parsley
- 1 kg (2 lb 4 oz) mackerel, cleaned and heads removed
- Cornish sea salt and freshly ground black pepper

TO SERVE

- Green Leaf Salad (see page 170)
- 1 lemon, cut into wedges

In a large bowl, combine 4 tablespoons of the olive oil with the lemon zest, garlic, 1 teaspoon of the chilli flakes, 1 tablespoon of the parsley, and some salt and pepper. Add the mackerel, toss to cover and leave to marinate for 30 minutes.

Meanwhile, fire up the barbecue.

Cook the marinated mackerel directly on the bars of the barbecue for 4–5 minutes until caramelised and charred (or use a griddle pan – just make sure it is really hot, as this will help the mackerel not stick).

Place on a warm serving plate and drizzle with the remaining 2 tablespoons of olive oil, and sprinkle with the remaining ½ teaspoon of chilli flakes and 1 tablespoon of parsley. Accompany with a green leaf salad and some lemon wedges.

COOK'S NOTE Sardines also work wonderfully over coals. If you don't have a barbecue, bake the fish in a hot oven. For even quicker cooking, ask your fishmonger to butterfly fillet the fish.

Salt-Baked Sea Bass, Herbs, Tarragon Mayo

A recipe inspired by the sea. This salt-baked bass is simple to make and will shine at any table. Sea bass has delicious depth of flavour and encasing it in Cornish sea salt gently wraps the fish up and locks in all the moisture and fragrance of the herbs and lemon as it cooks. Accompanied by tarragon mayo, fennel gratin and Cornish earlies, this will transport you to the coast – a fish supper like no other.

SERVES 4

2 egg whites
100 ml (3½ fl oz/scant ½ cup) water
1 kg (2 lb 4 oz/3½ cups) coarse Cornish sea salt
1 bunch of fresh-flat leaf parsley
1 bunch of fresh marjoram
1 bunch of fresh tarragon
1 fennel bulb with fronds, finely sliced
1 lemon, thinly sliced
1 x 1.5–2 kg (3 lb 5 oz–4 lb 8 oz) sea bass (from a sustainable source), gutted, gills removed, scales left on

FOR THE TARRAGON MAYO
3 egg yolks
1 teaspoon Dijon mustard
juice of 1 lemon
250ml (8½ fl oz/1 cup) sunflower oil
a handful of tarragon
Cornish sea salt and freshly ground black pepper

TO SERVE
boiled new potatoes
Green Leaf Salad (see page 170) or watercress

Preheat the oven to 200°C (180°C fan/400°F/Gas 6).

In a large bowl, whisk the egg whites until gently foaming. Combine with the measured water, then add the sea salt and mix. Evenly spread one-third of the salt mixture over a large baking sheet or tray.

Stuff the herbs, fennel and lemon slices into the cavity of the fish, then lay the fish on top of the salt. Be careful not to get the salt inside the cavity – you don't want to make the fish too salty. Encase everything but the head and tail of the fish in the salt, tucking it in tightly.

Bake in the oven for 35–40 minutes. To test if the bass is ready, push a skewer through the salt into the thickest part of the fish – if the skewer is warm and almost hot, it is ready. Remove from the oven and allow to rest for 15 minutes.

Meanwhile, make the tarragon mayo. Combine the egg yolks, mustard, lemon juice and a good pinch of sea salt in a food processor and whizz until just combined. With the motor still running, slowly pour the oil through the funnel in a fine, slow stream until it is all incorporated and has emulsified. Remove the tarragon leaves from their stalks and roughly chop (as you chop, the delicious fragrance will be released). Fold through the mayo and taste, adjusting the seasoning as needed.

Gently crack the salt casing and pull it away from the fish, brushing any excess salt from the top. Gently loosen and carefully transfer the fish to a large plate. Pull the skin away and use a round-ended knife to scrape away any darker fish, leaving you with beautifully cooked and tender sea bass.

Serve with tarragon mayo, new potatoes and a green salad or some watercress.

COOK'S NOTES I always use Cornish sea salt – so pure and natural. Those beautiful, microscopic, pyramid-shaped flakes are essential in my cooking. For a citrus version of the mayo, omit the tarragon and add the zest of 1 lemon and 1 lime.

Cornish Bouillabaisse

This is my dream fishy supper – a seaside soirée just would not be the same without this showstopper, which is also great as a Sunday lunch. Cook with your favourite tunes and glass in hand. Simple and quick to make, colourful and delicious, this rustic stew will always be a winner for satisfying seaside cravings. Use whatever fish and shellfish you like – I've used Cornish gurnard, mussels and prawns (shrimp) – to dress it up or down. I also make more aioli than is strictly necessary (see page 162) to celebrate this wonderful dish.

SERVES 4

4 tablespoons good olive oil, plus extra for drizzling
2 leeks, finely sliced
1 fennel bulb, finely sliced (discard tough outer layers and reserve the fronds)
4 garlic cloves, crushed
1 tablespoon tomato purée (paste)
1 pinch of saffron, steeped in a splash of warm water
a handful of basil leaves, plus extra to garnish
zest and juice of 1 orange
100 ml (3½ fl oz/scant ½ cup) Pernod or Noilly Prat vermouth
500 ml (17 fl oz/2 cups) fish stock
2 x 400 g (14 oz) tins of chopped tomatoes
1 kg (2 lb 4 oz) live mussels, cleaned (discard any that are still open)
4 gurnard fillets (skin on and filleted – ask your fishmonger), cut in half (cod or monkfish would be good replacements)
250 g (9 oz) shell-on prawns (shrimp)
Cornish sea salt and freshly ground black pepper

TO SERVE
slices of sourdough, toasted
Saffron Aioli (page 162)

Heat the olive oil in a large saucepan that has a lid over a medium heat, add the leeks, fennel and garlic, and sauté until softened, then add the tomato purée and stir gently for 2–3 minutes. Add the steeped saffron, basil, orange zest and juice, Pernod or vermouth, fish stock and chopped tomatoes, and simmer for 10–15 minutes, stirring occasionally.

Add the mussels to the sauce, cover the pan with the lid and cook for 5–6 minutes until they have opened. Remove the mussels with a slotted spoon (discard any unopened ones at this point) and set aside in a bowl.

Transfer the sauce to a food processor or blender and blitz until smooth, then pour the sauce back into a large clean pan and simmer uncovered for 8–10 minutes until reduced.

Meanwhile, remove most of the mussels from their shells, reserving a few in their shells for garnish (3 per person).

Season the sauce with some sea salt and black pepper, then place the gurnard fillets, skin-side up, into the sauce along with the prawns and cook for 3–4 minutes until the fish is cooked through and the prawns have turned pink. Finally, add the cooked mussels and mussels in their shells back to the pan to warm through.

Divide the bouillabaisse between four warm bowls and finish off with a few extra basil leaves, the reserved fennel fronds and drizzle of olive oil. Serve with sourdough croutons and saffron aioli.

COOK'S NOTE Keep this as sustainable and local as possible, talk to your fishmonger about what is best to use. Once upon a time, it seemed only good enough to use as bait in lobster and crab pots, but gurnard has made a comeback over the last few years. A white, firm-fleshed fish, it works so well in stews and is a great fish to batter for your Friday fish supper. I will always champion the gurnard.

Saffron Aioli

Earthy, floral and almost sweet, saffron is a very much used ingredient in my kitchen. As good in savoury dishes as sweet, giving a unique depth of flavour and colour, the deep yellow hue of the crocus flower is simply golden magic. Grown in Cornwall on the Roseland Peninsula, saffron has been a highly prized spice in the county over the years. This saffron aioli is moreish and lifts my fish stew recipe (see page 160) to new heights.

SERVES 6

3 free-range egg yolks
a squeeze of lemon juice
1 garlic clove, peeled
1 teaspoon Dijon mustard
a pinch of Cornish sea salt
200 ml (7 fl oz/scant 1 cup) sunflower oil
2 pinches of saffron steeped in 1 tablespoon hot water

Place the egg yolks in a food processor and add the lemon juice, garlic, mustard and a good pinch of sea salt. Whizz until just combined. Measure the sunflower oil into a jug, then – with the motor of the food processor still running – pour the oil slowly in through the funnel in a fine, slow stream until all of it is incorporated and it has emulsified.

Fold the steeped saffron through the mayo until you achieve a burnished golden hue (or the colour 'tarky', as I know it). Taste for seasoning and use immediately, or store in the refrigerator for up to 4 days.

COOK'S NOTE Avoid storing the saffron itself in the refrigerator. Instead, store it in a cool, dark place – a larder is ideal. Saffron is definitely one of my essential larder ingredients.

Anya Potato, Halloumi, Tomato, Chilli & Honey Rosemary Skewers

In my first book, *Sea & Shore*, I had a monkfish version of this recipe. Simply the best stack of flavours cooked over fire. Anya potatoes are my favourite to use in this vegetable-based variation, as they are waxy and slightly gnarly looking, but any waxy small new potato will do. The rosemary skewers add a lovely depth of flavour.

SERVES 6

- 750 g (1 lb 10 oz) Anya potatoes (or other small new potatoes), halved
- 200 g (7 oz) cherry tomatoes, halved crossways
- 2 x 250 g (9 oz) packs of halloumi, cut into 2 cm (¾ in) squares
- 4 tablespoons runny honey
- 4 tablespoons good olive oil, plus extra for drizzling
- 2½ teaspoons chilli (hot pepper) flakes
- zest and juice of 1 lemon
- 12 long woody stalks of fresh rosemary, plus extra leaves to serve
- Cornish sea salt and freshly ground black pepper
- lemon wedges, to serve

Fire up the barbecue while you prepare your ingredients.

Parboil the potatoes in a pan of boiling water until partially cooked and still holding their shape, then drain well.

Place the part-cooked new potatoes, tomatoes, halloumi, honey, olive oil, chilli flakes, lemon zest and juice, and a good pinch each of sea salt and black pepper in a large bowl. Toss to combine and leave to marinate for 10–15 minutes.

Thread the marinated ingredients alternately onto the woody rosemary skewers, allowing 2–3 pieces of each ingredient on each skewer (although this will depend on the length of your skewers).

Barbecue the skewers on all sides, keeping them moving for 5–6 minutes, until caramelised. Drizzle with more olive oil and any remaining marinade, and sprinkle with sea salt and extra rosemary leaves.

Lay the halloumi skewers on a warm serving dish and serve with the lemon wedges. I also like this with the miso-buttered corn on the cob on page 174.

COOK'S NOTE The halloumi chunks do have a tendency to break on the skewers when you are threading them, but persevere. Finding the woodiest stalks of rosemary will help. If using wooden skewers, soak them in water for 20 minutes beforehand.

Monkfish & Saffron Curry

My fish curry of dreams. Monkfish is very forgiving and great if you are new to fish cookery. I slightly undercook it so it is a little translucent, and resting it before eating is always a good idea. Monkfish is so robust and meaty, yet with a delicate flavour, it stands up very well to the gentle spices here. Serve with rice, or it is delicious with quinoa.

SERVES 6

1 teaspoon saffron
juice of ½ lime
250 g (9 oz) fine green beans, topped, tailed and cut in half
1 tablespoon good olive oil
1 bunch of spring onions (scallions), trimmed and sliced
2 garlic cloves, chopped
5 mm (¼ in) piece of fresh root ginger, finely grated
1 red chilli, finely sliced
2 curry leaves
2 teaspoons ground turmeric
1 teaspoon ground coriander
450 g (1 lb) monkfish, trimmed and cut into 4 cm (1¾ in) pieces
1 x 400 g (14 oz) tin of coconut milk
125 ml (4 fl oz/½ cup) fish stock
4 tablespoons roughly chopped fresh coriander (cilantro), to garnish

In a small bowl, add the saffron to the lime juice and leave to steep while you cook.

Briefly blanch the green beans in a pan of boiling water, then drain and refresh under cold running water or in a bowl of iced water, so they retain their green colour. Set aside.

Heat the olive oil in a heavy-based pan over a medium-low heat, add the spring onions and sauté until softened, then stir in the garlic, ginger and chilli. Add the curry leaves and ground spices, and cook, stirring, for 1 minute, then add the monkfish pieces and cook for 2–3 minutes on each side. Add the coconut milk and steeped saffron, and simmer over a low heat for 10 minutes, then stir in the blanched green beans.

Serve in bowls garnished with coriander.

COOK'S NOTE You are looking for a burnished yellow sauce here, so simmer low and slow. I find myself spooning the rice or quinoa directly onto my curry when I come to serve it in bowls – this allows the sauce to be soaked up. Always so good the next day, if you have leftovers.

Ratatouille

I can remember my grandmother Marnie at her kitchen table preparing the colourful array of vegetables: aubergines (eggplant), courgettes (zucchini), (bell) peppers and tomatoes. Delicious summery flavours, layered with good olive oil, garlic, red onion and herbs. A perfect accompaniment for so many dishes, or a meal in itself with a green salad. Apart from the name of this dish also being that of my favourite Disney film (so good), this recipe is rustic and colourful and can be made throughout the year.

SERVES 4

2 red onions
2 aubergines (eggplant)
2 courgettes (zucchini)
2 red (bell) peppers
4 tablespoons good olive oil
2 garlic cloves, chopped
1 teaspoon cayenne pepper
2 x 400 g (14 oz) tins of cherry tomatoes
100 g (3½ oz) fresh coriander (cilantro), chopped, plus extra to serve
100 g (3½ oz) flat-leaf parsley, chopped, plus extra to serve
Cornish sea salt and freshly ground black pepper

First, your *mise en place* (get all your vegetables ready to go). Peel and cut the red onions into wedges. Trim the aubergines and courgettes, and cut into 3 cm (1¼ in) chunks. Deseed and chop the peppers.

Heat a large pan with 2 tablespoons of the olive oil, add the aubergines, courgettes and peppers, and cook (in batches, if necessary) until softened and golden. Remove with a slotted spoon to a bowl and set aside.

Add the onions, garlic and cayenne pepper to the pan and cook until softened, then add the aubergines, courgettes and peppers back into the pan and stir through. Add the tinned tomatoes, coriander, parsley and the remaining 2 tablespoons of olive oil, season with sea salt and black pepper, then cover and simmer for 25–30 minutes until reduced, sweet and delicious.

Garnish with extra herbs, to serve.

COOK'S NOTE Serve on its own with yoghurt and rice, or it makes a perfect accompaniment to a roasted Butterfly Leg of Lamb (see page 194).

Green Leaf Salad

Eat your greens. There are so many varieties of salad leaves and I love nothing more than a salad of greens. Little gem, romaine, frissé, rocket (arugula), round lettuce, sorrel and spinach ... For me, I always keep it green. An addition of thinly sliced spring onions (scallions), avocado, cucumber (skin off) and some toasted pine nuts with a lemon dressing is just perfect. Don't hold back, make your salad whatever you want it to be. Here is a recipe for a simple, yet yummy, green leaf salad.

SERVES 4

- 1 round lettuce
- 2 little gem lettuce
- 4 spring onions (scallions), trimmed
- 1 cucumber, peeled
- 2 small ripe avocados
- juice of 1 lemon
- 3 tablespoons extra virgin olive oil
- 50 g (2 oz/⅓ cup) toasted pine nuts
- Cornish sea salt and freshly ground black pepper

Prepare your leaves: wash them in a colander and dry off (placing them gently in a clean dish towel is how I do this). Arrange the leaves in your favourite salad bowl.

Thinly slice the spring onions and cucumber, and add the slices to the leaves.

Carefully cut all the way around each avocado lengthways, going as deep as the stones. Hold each avocado in your hands and twist until you can pull the two halves apart. Pull out and discard the stones and use a teaspoon to help you scoop the avocado flesh out into nice half rounds. Add to the salad.

In a bowl, mix the lemon juice and good olive oil together with a pinch of sea salt and a couple of grinds of pepper. Mix into the salad and serve immediately, sprinkled with the toasted pine nuts.

COOK'S NOTE Edible flowers are so beautiful to add through your leaves to give a pop of colour: try nasturtiums, borage, violas and amaranth, to name but a few.

Seaweed Butter

Beautiful, delicious and rich in vitamins and minerals, Cornish seaweeds – purslane, rock samphire and sea beets – can be found plentifully by the shore. Seaweed butter is the most wonderful addition to fish and vegetable recipes. Naturally salty, it is delicious melted over scallops or lobster. It can be made and sliced in advance and freezes beautifully.

MAKES 150 G (5 OZ)

- 5 g (¼ oz) sea lettuce (washed and dried)
- 150 g (5 oz) unsalted butter, softened

Place the washed, dried sea lettuce on a baking tray and dehydrate it in a very low oven overnight.

The next day, grind the sea lettuce down in a pestle and mortar to a soft powder, then stir it through the softened butter. Place the butter onto a square of kitchen foil placed over a sheet of cling film (plastic wrap). Roll both layers around the butter until it forms a log, then twist the ends to seal like a cracker. Chill in the refrigerator until firm, then slice into rounds. Use as needed.

COOK'S NOTES Sea lettuce can be foraged from the beach. When foraging, you need to know what you are looking for; if you don't, make sure you find out from someone who does. Otherwise, good-quality sea lettuce can be bought online. Frozen butter slices will keep for up to 1 month.

Garlic & Flat-Leaf Parsley Butter

A classic combination. Is there anything better than homemade garlic bread to share? I also use this to spread over sweetcorn cooked over hot coals (see page 174).

MAKES 200 G (7 OZ)

- 200 g (7 oz) unsalted butter, softened
- 4 garlic cloves, crushed
- 1 teaspoon Cornish sea salt
- 4 tablespoons chopped flat-leaf parsley (stalks and all, as they are sweet)

Place the softened butter in a bowl and beat until pale and creamy. Add the garlic, salt and chopped parsley, and mix in. Roll the butter into a log, as decribed above, then chill in the refrigerator until firm. Slice into rounds and use as needed.

COOK'S NOTES For extra caramelised sweetness, roast the garlic beforehand. For Tarragon Butter, the same quantity of chopped tarragon also works a treat in place of the parsley.

Corn on the Cob, Chilli, Miso Butter

I love corn on the cob. Here, I keep the husks on and rub them with olive oil and sea salt, cook them over coals and then drown them in a delicious butter of white miso, chilli, lime juice and zest, and finish with fresh coriander (cilantro). The miso butter is so delicious and totally life-enhancing.

SERVES 4

- 4 whole corn on the cob, husks on
- 4 tablespoons olive oil
- 250 g (9 oz) unsalted butter, softened
- 1 tablespoon white miso paste
- 2 teaspoons chilli (hot pepper) flakes, plus extra to garnish
- zest and juice of 2 limes
- 1 small bunch of fresh coriander (cilantro), leaves roughly chopped
- Cornish sea salt and freshly ground black pepper

Fire up the barbecue or preheat the oven to 200°C (180°C fan/400°F/Gas 6) while you prepare your ingredients.

Place the corn into a deep baking tray, pull back some of the husks to expose the corn and rub with the olive oil and season well with sea salt. Replace the husks.

Cook over the coals for 15 minutes, or in the hot oven, until gently charred and cooked through.

Meanwhile, place the butter, miso paste, chilli flakes, lime zest and juice, and a pinch each of sea salt and black pepper into a food processor and blitz until smooth. Fold in most of the roughly chopped coriander, reserving a little for garnish.

Melt the miso butter gently in a pan, pull back the husks once again, then pour the hot butter over the cooked corn.

Serve sprinkled with extra chilli flakes and the reserved coriander.

COOK'S NOTE Butter is the important ingredient here. Drown the sweetcorn in butter, whether it is miso butter; nasturtium, chilli and lime; tarragon or seaweed butter. Flavoured butters can be made in advance, chilled, then sliced and frozen so they are always on hand (see page 172).

Simple Tomato Salad, Basil

Growing up, I used to help Mr Bone in the garden. He was a wonderful character and a very good gardener, and etched in my mind forever is the smell of the vines in the greenhouse and of tasting ripe tomatoes picked straight from them. Any tomato can be used for this recipe, but the larger beef tomatoes work particularly well. Slice thinly and arrange on a plate with basil and thyme leaves, good olive oil and a dose of sunshine (if possible).

SERVES 4

- 4 beef tomatoes, at room temperature
- 1 bunch of fresh basil, leaves only
- 1 bunch of fresh thyme, soft leaves only
- 2 tablespoons cider vinegar
- 4 tablespoons good olive oil
- Cornish sea salt and freshly ground black pepper

Slice the beef tomatoes and layer with most of the basil and thyme leaves on your favourite plate. Season with sea salt.

Whisk together the vinegar and olive oil, then drizzle over the tomatoes just 15 minutes before serving the salad. Tear over more basil and thyme, and season with more salt and black pepper.

COOK'S NOTE Always store tomatoes at room temperature (cold tomatoes are just wrong) and handle with care. Although tomatoes, like many ingredients, can be bought all year round these days, there is nothing more delicious than a ripe summer tomato.

Raspberry Ripple Ice Cream

As a child I have fond memories of Neapolitan ice cream, which came in a rectangular block, Funny Feet and the classic Mivvi ice lollies, but my favourite flavour will always be raspberry ripple. It is so, so good. I make a vanilla base with real vanilla, gently roast the raspberries, then blend and sieve, layering the resulting raspberry purée with the softly churned vanilla ice cream. Ideal served in cones or simply scooped into a bowl. I would always stir my ice cream round and round, and eat it with great happiness.

SERVES 6

RASPBERRY PURÉE
- 500 g (1 lb 2 oz) raspberries
- 2 tablespoons caster (superfine) sugar
- 2 tablespoons crème de cassis

VANILLA ICE CREAM BASE
- 350 ml (12 fl oz/generous 1⅓ cups) milk
- 400 ml (13 fl oz/generous 1½ cups) double (heavy) cream
- 1 vanilla pod, split
- 6 free-range egg yolks
- 125 g (4 oz/generous ½ cup) caster (superfine) sugar

For the raspberry purée, preheat the oven to 190°C (170°C fan/375°F/Gas 5).

Place the raspberries in a roasting tray and shake over the 2 tablespoons of sugar. Roast in the oven for 8–10 minutes until soft and juicy.

Transfer to a food processor and blitz to a smooth purée, then pass through a fine mesh sieve to remove the pips. Add the crème de cassis, then set aside to cool. Cover and store in the refrigerator while you make the ice-cream base.

For the vanilla ice-cream base, pour the milk and cream into a heavy-based pan and add the split vanilla pod. Slowly bring to simmering point, then turn off the heat and leave to infuse for 10 minutes. Strain through a fine mesh sieve into a clean pan.

In a separate large pan, whisk together the egg yolks and sugar, then pour in the warm cream mixture, stirring continuously. Place back on the stove and heat gently until it begins to thicken or you can run your finger through it on the back of a wooden spoon and your finger leaves a trail. Allow to cool, then cover and refrigerate overnight.

The next day, churn the ice-cream base in an ice-cream maker until thick and creamy, according to the manufacturer's instructions. I use a Magimix Gelato Expert ice-cream machine on the ice cream setting. Spoon a third of the mixture into a container, then spoon over a layer of raspberry purée and gently swirl it into the base mixture. Repeat this process twice more, each time marbling the purée gently into the ice cream. Freeze for 3–5 hours or overnight.

Serve scooped into cones or bowls. For something a little different, mini cones work beautifully as a little petit four, although one is never enough.

COOK'S NOTE The gelato setting on an ice-cream machine works beautifully too, giving you a light and airy ice cream. Swap out the raspberries for blackberries, blackcurrants or strawberries.

Roasted Stone Fruit

Whatever the season, stone fruits always remind me of sunshiney days. Peaches, apricots, mangoes, cherries and greengages for lighter days, and – as summer slips into autumn – the arrival of plums. Stone fruits are simply lovely eaten when perfectly ripe. I also love them roasted into pies, crumbles, compôtes and jams, preserving them throughout the year. Roasting them in Marsala wine makes them feel extra special, particularly when served with a dollop of crème fraîche.

SERVES 4

- 3 peaches, halved and stoned (pitted)
- 3 nectarines, halved and stoned (pitted)
- 6 apricots, halved and stoned (pitted)
- 100 g (3½ oz) cherries, halved and stoned (pitted)
- 3 bay leaves
- 1 vanilla pod, split lengthways
- 400 ml (13 fl oz/generous 1½ cups) Marsala wine
- 2 tablespoons honey
- 20 g (¾ oz) unsalted butter

Preheat the oven to 200°C (180°C fan/400°F/Gas 6).

Toss all the fruits, bay leaves and the vanilla pod into a snug ovenproof dish or roasting tin (pan). Pour over the Marsala, drizzle over the honey and dot with the butter.

Roast for 30 minutes until the fruits are juicy and tender but not mushy. Serve warm.

COOK'S NOTE This roasted compôte of fruits is lovely for breakfast or served warm with clotted ice cream (see page 214).

Sunday

(TIME TOGETHER)

Lazy

Lunch

SEASHELL whites. Nothing says more about a weekend than Sunday lunch. I will sometimes plan my entire week around what our Sunday is going to look like; it can be that beacon of light in any week. Let's talk about lunchtime. I love to eat lunch, always a natural break in the day, a time to refuel – whatever you are doing or celebrating. There is no denying that long lunches are the best, followed by a seaside walk and then a siesta (perfectly acceptable). I have in recent months become busier and busier at work, so Sundays have become an important day to me. A day for rebooting, recharging and always cooking.

In this chapter, I share the recipes that I cook a lot for family and friends throughout the year. I am a home bird, preferring to stay *chez moi* to potter and prepare lunch, usually a late lunch, for my children, family and friends. Good wine, a simple table and flowers or cuttings from my garden whatever the season. Eating together is, in my view, essential, medicinal. A time for feeling grateful and being in the now and not thinking too far ahead. Slowing right down and enjoying the simple chores of life. A chore does not have to be a chore – it is how you approach it that matters. So, whatever your Sunday plans are, spend them with love.

Potted Shrimp

A very civilised thing, potted shrimps are in my view a one-pot snack. Perfect as a quick lunch on-the-go or for a picnic by the sea. All that's needed is some good bread and a knife to spread. Delicious.

SERVES 4

200 g (7 oz) unsalted butter
350 g (12 oz) brown shrimps (miniature shrimp)
juice of 1 lemon
a grating of fresh nutmeg
1 teaspoon cayenne pepper
1 large bay leaf, plus 4 small bay leaves to garnish

Melt half of the butter in a medium pan, then stir in the shrimps, lemon juice, nutmeg, cayenne pepper and the large bay leaf and allow to cool.

When cool, remove and discard the large bay leaf. Divide the shrimp mixture among four small ramekins and press down gently, making sure you have an equal measure of butter just submerging the shrimps.

Melt the remaining butter and clarify (see Cook's note). Spoon the clarified butter over the top of each ramekin to create a seal on top of the shrimps and gently place a small bay leaf in the top of each. Place in the refrigerator to cool and set.

Remove from the refrigerator 10–15 minutes before serving.

COOK'S NOTE To clarify butter, melt the butter in a pan over a low heat. Skim off the froth, then carefully pour the clear liquid into a bowl, leaving behind the milky part. Clarified butter also makes delicious warm vinaigrettes (butter, plus a little sugar and vinegar to taste), which go perfectly with steamed or baked fish.

Cornish Crab Cakes

Cornwall would not be Cornwall without crab. Perfect rounds of delicious crab, gently pan-fried until golden brown, these fish cakes are slightly lighter as they are potato-less. Accompany with a green salad and some citrus mayo.

SERVES 4

500 g (1 lb 2 oz) mixed white crab meat, picked
zest and juice of 1 lemon
4 spring onions (scallions), very thinly sliced
1 tablespoon chopped chives
2 tablespoons crème fraîche
4 tablespoons plain (all-purpose) flour, plus extra for dusting
2 medium free-range eggs, lightly beaten
100 g (3½ oz/1¼ cups) fresh white breadcrumbs
25 g (1 oz) unsalted butter
4 tablespoons sunflower oil
Cornish sea salt and freshly ground black pepper

TO SERVE
Citrus Mayo (see variation to Tarragon Mayo, page 158)
Green Leaf Salad (see page 170)
lemon wedges

Put the crab meat in a mixing bowl along with the lemon zest and juice, spring onions, chives, and some salt and pepper. Mix together, adding the crème fraîche to help bind the mixture. Dust your hands with flour and divide the mixture into 8 round shapes, each about 2 cm (¾ in) thick. Place on a plate and chill in the refrigerator for 1 hour.

Put the flour on a plate and season well, pour the beaten eggs into a shallow dish, then scatter the breadcrumbs on a separate plate. Take a chilled crab cake and dip it into the flour, coating it on both sides, then dip it into the egg and finally the breadcrumbs. Set aside and repeat with the rest of the crab cakes.

Heat the butter and oil in a large frying pan (skillet) over a medium heat. To test if the oil is hot enough, place a breadcrumb or two into the oil; if it immediately turns golden brown, the oil is ready (do not leave unattended). Add the crab cakes to the pan (in batches) and fry for 3–4 minutes until crisp and golden brown underneath. Turn them over and cook for another 2–3 minutes until golden brown. Remove with a slotted spoon to a plate lined with paper towels and keep warm while you cook the rest.

Serve with a green salad and dollops of citrus mayo, sprinkled with a little sea salt and with lemon wedges on the side.

COOK'S NOTE Make your crab cakes bite-size for a drinks party (yes, an old-fashioned drinks party) and top with mayo and a small sprig of watercress.

gardens open to the public on certain
days of the year. For more information
www.leckfordestate.co.uk

Butterflied Leg of Lamb Roasted over Coals with Lemon, Garlic & Thyme

This is a wonderful way to cook lamb in the oven or over coals. Splitting the joint effectively into a butterfly shape allows it to cook more quickly and evenly (the butcher can prepare the joint for you). This is such a zesty marinade for the lamb and I think it works best if left to marinate overnight. Serve with Tzatziki in warmer weather (see opposite) or with Damson and Plum Jam (see page 240) in the colder months. Pictured overleaf.

SERVES 6

2–2.5 kg (4 lb 8 oz–5 lb 8 oz) leg of lamb (weight before butterflying – ask your butcher to butterfly the lamb for you)
Cornish sea salt and freshly ground black pepper
Damson and Plum Jam (see page 240) or Tzatziki (see opposite), to serve

FOR THE MARINADE
zest and juice of 3 lemons
1 tablespoon Dijon mustard
4 garlic cloves, crushed
3 tablespoons runny honey
2–3 tablespoons good olive oil
2 small bunches of thyme, leaves removed from stalks

Mix the marinade ingredients in a large bowl. Add the butterflied lamb to the bowl and rub the marinade all over the meat. Refrigerate for at least 3 hours, or even better overnight.

Bring the lamb back to room temperature before cooking. Remove from the marinade and season with sea salt and freshly ground black pepper.

Fire up the barbecue. When hot enough, cook the lamb over the hot coals for 45 minutes, turning it from time to time (or see Cook's note for oven roasting).

Transfer the lamb to a board and allow it to rest for 15 minutes before slicing and serving.

In the spring and summer, serve with dollops of Tzatziki (see opposite), more lemon wedges and a green leaf salad. Alternatively, in autumn or winter, serve with my Damson and Plum Jam and potato dauphinoise (see page 208) or some baby roast potatoes.

COOK'S NOTE To cook the lamb in the oven, preheat it to 220°C (200°C fan/430°F/Gas 8). Place the lamb in a roasting pan and roast for 15 minutes per 450 g (1 lb), then give it an extra 15 minutes. Baste the meat with the pan juices every 15 minutes.

Tzatziki

Bringing some sunshine to your Sunday lunch whatever the weather. There is something so delicious about cucumber, yoghurt, crème fraîche, garlic, green herbs and citrus. This goes perfectly with the rich lamb opposite.

SERVES 6

- 1 small cucumber
- 2 garlic cloves, crushed
- 2 tablespoons good olive oil, plus extra for drizzling
- 250 g (9 oz/1 cup) Greek yoghurt
- 250 g (9 oz/1 cup) crème fraîche
- 1 small bunch of dill, finely chopped
- 1 small bunch of garden mint, finely chopped
- 1 lemon, halved, for squeezing
- Cornish sea salt and freshly ground black pepper

Skin and deseed the cucumber and grate it. Place the grated cucumber in a fine mesh sieve set over a bowl, lightly salt it and leave for 1 hour to drain, stirring occasionally to help sieve the liquid out.

In a small bowl, combine the garlic, olive oil, yoghurt and crème fraîche, and fold together. Pat the cucumber dry in a dish towel, then mix it in with the other ingredients. Add most of the dill and mint, a squeeze of lemon juice and some salt and pepper, then taste and adjust.

To serve, drizzle with extra olive oil and more herbs.

Fillet of Beef, Horseradish Cream, Pumpkin, Red Onions

A time for celebration and being together. Undeniably luxurious, sometimes only beef fillet will do. This is a wonderful way to gently cook the beef, but always allow good resting time. I love the colours of the pumpkin, red onions, rosemary and garlic with dollops of horseradish clotted cream. This is a dish that will bring much happiness to your table and leftovers make the most delicious beef sandwiches.

SERVES 6, WITH LEFTOVERS

1.5 kg (3 lb 5 oz) beef fillet, trimmed (ask your butcher)
4 tablespoons olive oil
6 garlic cloves, skin on
6–8 sprigs of rosemary
100 g (3½ oz) unsalted butter
Cornish sea salt and freshly ground black pepper

FOR THE RED ONIONS
2 tablespoons vegetable oil
2 large red onions, quartered
6 sprigs of rosemary, leaves finely chopped
6 juniper berries, crushed
1 star anise
2 cloves

FOR THE PUMPKIN
1 small pumpkin, peeled, deseeded, sliced into small rustic pieces
1 tablespoon plain (all-purpose) flour
500 ml (17 fl oz/2 cups) vegetable stock
100 ml (3½ fl oz/scant ½ cup) white wine
a few sprigs of flat-leaf parsley, finely chopped, to garnish

HORSERADISH CREAM
200 g (7 oz/2 cups) crème fraîche
2 tablespoons Dijon mustard
juice of 1 lemon
50 g (2 oz) fresh horseradish, peeled and grated

Preheat the oven to 100°C (80°C fan/225°F/Gas ¼).

Lay out some ovenproof cling film (plastic wrap) on a clean, dry work surface. Place the beef along the long edge of the cling film and roll it up tightly, holding both ends so it forms a cracker shape. Place in a roasting pan and cook in the oven for 1½ hours.

Remove the beef from the oven, then remove and discard the cling film. Heat a frying pan (skillet) until hot, add 2 tablespoons of the olive oil, then place the beef in the pan and fry for no more than 5–6 minutes, turning occasionally, until browned on all sides. Add the whole garlic cloves and rosemary sprigs, then add the remaining olive oil and the butter. When foaming, spoon it enthusiastically over the beef for 5–10 minutes to lock in all the delicious flavours. Turn off the heat and allow the beef to rest for 15 minutes in the pan (these timings allow for medium rare).

Meanwhile, prepare the red onions. Heat the oil in a pan over a low heat, add the onions and cook until softened, then add the rosemary, juniper berries, star anise and cloves. Never rush an onion, give them time to soften and sweeten. Once softened, remove the spices to serve.

Cook the pumpkin in a saucepan of simmering water for 5 minutes, then drain off the water, sprinkle over the flour and stir to cook out the flour. Pour in the stock and wine, bring to the boil, then reduce to a simmer for 20 minutes until all is tender. Season to taste and garnish with the parsley.

For the horseradish cream, mix together the crème fraîche, mustard and lemon juice with a whisk. Add the grated horseradish, then season and taste.

Remove the beef to a carving board, slice it thickly and serve with the rosemary and garlic, horseradish cream, pumpkin and red onions. Some greens also work well here.

COOK'S NOTE Horseradish is from the mustard family, so may make your eyes water (similar to onions). If you cannot find fresh horseradish, add 2 tablespoons of store-bought horseradish to the crème fraîche. Pumpkin could be replaced with butternut squash.

Coq au Vin

A glossy, one-pot, red wine supper, rustic and served straight from my old favourite Le Creuset pan, this evokes nostalgia for the time I lived in France and cooked in a restaurant in Burgundy. Full of flavour and charm, and in the past considered peasant food, chicken in red wine is always a winner for me.

SERVES 4

- 2 tablespoons good olive oil
- 50 g (2 oz) unsalted butter
- 100 g (3½ oz) smoked bacon, cut into lardons
- 12 small shallots, peeled
- 150 g (5 oz) chestnut (cremini) mushrooms, sliced
- 1.5 kg (3 lb 5 oz) chicken, jointed
- 3 tablespoons brandy
- 2 tablespoons plain (all-purpose) flour
- 100 ml (3½ fl oz/scant ½ cup) chicken stock
- 600 ml (20 fl oz/2½ cups) red wine
- bouquet garni of bay, rosemary and thyme
- a pinch of fresh nutmeg
- Cornish sea salt and freshly ground black pepper
- 4 tablespoons chopped flat-leaf parsley, to garnish

Preheat the oven to 200°C (180°C fan/400°F/Gas 6).

Heat 1 tablespoon of the olive oil and 25 g (1 oz) of the butter in a large heavy-based saucepan that has a lid over a medium-low heat. Add the bacon lardons and shallots, and cook until golden brown. Do this slowly so the onions do not burn and become bitter. Add the remaining olive oil and butter to the pan, then add the mushrooms and cook until golden. Remove from the pan with a slotted spoon and set aside.

Place the pieces of chicken in the pan, skin-side down, and cook until golden brown. Add the brandy to flambé briefly and deglaze the pan, stirring up all the delicious flavours from the bottom of the pan. Remove the chicken from the pan and set aside.

Sprinkle the flour into the pan and cook out for 2–3 minutes, stirring all the time. Add the chicken stock gradually, followed by the red wine and cook until slightly thickened. Place the chicken pieces back in the pan, skin-side up, along with the bacon, mushrooms and shallots. Add the bouquet garni, fresh nutmeg, some black pepper and a little sea salt (the bacon will already add some saltiness to the dish). Cover with a cartouche (a circle of damp greaseproof paper) and the pan lid and cook in the oven for about 1 hour.

Before serving, check the sauce for seasoning. Serve straight from the pan with chopped flat-leaf parsley to finish and mashed potatoes or bread – perfect to mop up all the delicious sauce.

COOK'S NOTE The wine must be good quality, robust and delicious, without being anything too expensive. Don't forget a glass for the cook.

Watercress & Keen's Cheddar Soufflé

Be brave, be bold. My mother would often make a twice-baked soufflé for the wonderful dinner parties that she used to throw when living and working in France, so I became very fond of a soufflé, savoury or sweet. I am also very fond of cheese and really in this recipe you can feel free to swap the Cheddar out for Gruyère, Gouda or Parmesan. Don't delay, eat straightaway.

SERVES 6

- 30 g (1 oz) salted butter, plus a little extra melted for greasing
- 100 g (3½ oz) watercress
- 30 g (1 oz) plain (all-purpose) flour
- 1 teaspoon English mustard
- 250 ml (8½ fl oz/1 cup) milk
- a grating of fresh nutmeg
- 6 medium free-range eggs, separated
- 200 g (7 oz) Keen's Cheddar (or good medium Cheddar), grated
- Cornish sea salt and freshly ground black pepper

Preheat the oven to 220°C (200°C fan/425°F/Gas 7). Butter six ramekins with melted butter and leave in the refrigerator while you prepare the soufflé.

Wash and dry the watercress, removing any tough stalks. Bring a pan of water to the boil and blanch the watercress for about 30 seconds, then immediately plunge it into ice-cold water to refresh it and retain its bright green colour. Drain and pat dry, then set aside.

Melt the butter in a pan over a medium heat, add the flour and the mustard and cook out for 1–2 minutes, stirring all the time. Slowly add the milk, whisking continuously, until thickened and glossy. Add a grating of nutmeg and check for seasoning, then remove from the heat and stir in the egg yolks and cheese.

In a clean dry bowl, whisk the egg whites until stiff, then fold into the sauce along with the watercress, being careful not to over-fold and lose all the air.

Carefully spoon the soufflé mixture into each ramekin, allowing a 1 cm (½ in) gap at the top. Bake on the middle shelf of the oven for 15–20 minutes until risen and golden brown.

Serve immediately and wonder why you do not make soufflés more often.

COOK'S NOTE Make sure your oven racks are arranged so that the soufflé has room to rise. Do not be tempted to open the oven during cooking – just let it work its magic.

Baked Salmon, Clementines, Citrus Vodka Glaze, Roasted Fennel

Clementines transport me to my childhood days and the promise of Christmas – they sing December to me, piled in a bowl in my kitchen or dropped into the bottom of my children's stockings. I love them in cakes, sorbets, jellies, jams or, as here, baked with a delicious whole salmon fillet with citrus vodka and honey, roasted with fennel that turns sweet and caramelised. Serve with dollops of dill crème fraîche. Often overlooked as an option to serve at Christmas, this salmon will make a wonderful, colourful and delicious centrepiece for your festive table, especially with some red cabbage on the side.

SERVES 6–8

FOR THE SALMON

- 4 tablespoons olive oil
- 1 kg (2 lb 4 oz) whole salmon fillet, pin boned
- 1–2 teaspoons chilli (hot pepper) flakes
- 4 tablespoons chopped dill
- 1 teaspoon pink peppercorns, crushed
- a pinch of Cornish sea salt
- 2 fennel bulbs with fronds
- 2 tablespoons lemon juice

FOR THE GLAZE

- zest and juice of 4 clementines or 2 oranges
- 100 ml (3½ fl oz/scant ½ cup) citrus vodka (see Cook's note)
- 6 tablespoons runny honey
- 3 star anise
- 3 bay leaves
- 3 clementines, unpeeled and cut into thin slices

FOR THE DILL CRÈME FRAÎCHE

- 500 g (1 lb 2 oz/2 cups) crème fraîche
- 4 tablespoons finely chopped dill, plus extra to garnish
- 1 tablespoon lemon juice
- Cornish sea salt and freshly ground pepper

Preheat the oven to 220°C (200°C fan/425°F/Gas 7). Line a baking tray with baking parchment and brush it with olive oil.

Place the salmon on the prepared tray, skin-side down. Brush the salmon with more olive oil and season with the chilli flakes, dill, crushed pink peppercorns and sea salt.

Trim the fennel, remove any tough outer layers and cut into thin slices with the fronds. Place in a bowl and toss with the remaining olive oil, lemon juice and more sea salt. Place the dressed fennel around the salmon ready to bake.

Make the dill crème fraîche by mixing all the ingredients together in a bowl with plenty of sea salt and black pepper. Always taste and consider.

To make the glaze, put the clementine zest, juice, vodka, honey, star anise and bay leaves in a pan and simmer until reduced by half. Add the sliced clementines and simmer for a further 5 minutes until softened. Remove the clementine slices and set aside. Reduce the sauce until glossy, then pour it over the salmon fillet.

Bake the salmon and fennel in the oven for 10 minutes, then remove from the oven and lay the candied clementine slices down the centre of the fillet. Return to the oven to bake for another 10 minutes.

Serve as a centrepiece on your table, with the dill crème fraîche on the side.

COOK'S NOTES When buying salmon, opt for sustainable wild salmon. If not available, organic farmed salmon is the next best thing. Most of the salmon we buy in the UK is from Scotland. I make a citrus vodka in collaboration with Colwith Farm Distillery. For later, a classic vodka martini with a twist to sip is simply always a good thing (see page 220).

Dauphinoise with Spinach & Clotted Cream

All that is comforting. Layers of potato interleaved with clotted cream, spinach, a hint of garlic and nutmeg. A dish that will bring you together with people you love. Wild garlic is a perfect replacement for the spinach, when it is in season. I am wild about wild garlic. To me, it is an essential springtime ingredient foraged from the woodlands. It has a subtle fragrance and works in pesto, risottos, pasta, scones and here in this delicious dauphinoise.

SERVES 8

- 50 g (2 oz) unsalted butter
- 300 g (10½ oz/1½ cups) clotted cream
- 150 ml (5 fl oz/scant ⅔ cup) crème fraîche or Rodda's double (heavy) cream
- 1 whole nutmeg, for grating
- 1.2 kg (2 lb 10 oz) waxy potatoes, peeled (Desirée potatoes work well)
- 900 ml (30 fl oz/3½ cups) full-fat milk
- 2 bay leaves
- 1 garlic clove, halved lengthways
- 200 g (7 oz) baby spinach, washed and stalks removed (wild garlic is a perfect alternative when in season)
- Cornish sea salt and freshly ground black pepper

Preheat the oven to 160°C (140°C fan/320°F/Gas 2). Grease the sides and bottom of an oven-to-table dish with a little of the butter and set the rest aside to use later.

Place the clotted cream and crème fraîche in a bowl and stir together, then add a pinch of sea salt, some black pepper and a grating of nutmeg.

Cut the potatoes into 2.5 mm (⅛ in) slices. Place them in a heavy-based pan and cover with the milk, then add a good pinch of sea salt, another grating of nutmeg, the bay leaves and garlic. Bring to the boil and cook for 10 minutes (be careful – the bottom of the pan can catch). Drain, discarding the milk, garlic and bay leaves.

Carefully layer the potatoes in the buttered dish alternating them with layers of spinach, seasoning each layer with salt and pepper. Make sure the top and bottom layers are just potato. Pour over the clotted cream mixture, making sure the top layer is just covered. Finish the top off with some more grated nutmeg and a few knobs of the remaining butter.

Bake in the middle of the oven for 1 hour, or until golden brown and a table knife passes through with ease. Allow to rest.

This is delicious with a leafy salad, on its own, or served as an accompaniment to my slow-roasted lamb (see page 194).

COOK'S NOTE A mandoline is a useful tool here to slice your potatoes (just be careful). If you want to enrich it even more and turn it into a gratin, grate 100 g (3½ oz) of Comte or Gruyère cheese over the top before baking.

Fromage Always (before pudding)

Cheese – a course always dear to my heart. Cheese or pudding first (that is the question)? For me, it just depends on whether I feel I want to eat something sweet first. Papa always taught me cheese first, to finish the red wine, which is very civilised, but sometimes cheese after pudding feels more indulgent and joyful. Whatever and however you like it, say yes to cheese. This is my perfect cheese board, served with oat crackers, figs, grapes, damson jelly and chutney:

MONTGOMERY CHEDDAR is rich and strong and almost melts in your mouth. I love a good Cheddar and this one never disappoints.

TICKLEMORE is a goats' cheese that is not goaty and always has a place on my cheese board. Figs baked with honey, thyme and Ticklemore is one of my go-to quick suppers that always delights.

TUNWORTH – oh Tunworth – you are truly delicious, rich, creamy and unctuous. Pile it high on an oat biscuit with softened set honey and thyme.

HELFORD BLUE is a soft, creamy, subtly blue artisan Cornish cheese. A gold award-winner, as is Helford White, which is another delicious cheese from Treveador Farm Dairy in Cornwall.

COOK'S NOTE Cheese is always a comfort as much as it is a delight. My go-to snack is a humble piece of Cheddar and a Pink Lady apple – or cheese on toast, usually made on a Sunday night, with Worcestershire sauce and a side of ketchup, it definitely warms my heart. A life without cheese would not be a life at all.

Treacle Tart

Golden syrup deliciousness and the sweeter the better, this is a favourite pudding in our house. It brings back memories of my childhood and treacle tart for Sunday lunch, as this was always one of my mother's signature puddings. The right balance of syrup to crumbs is essential here. Not enough and the filling will be dry and chewy; too much and it will not set. Thank you Pippa for the apple tip off – simply wonderful. More tart please!

SERVES 6–8

FOR THE SWEET PASTRY

125 g (4 oz) unsalted butter, cold and diced
250 g (9 oz/2 cups) plain (all-purpose) flour, plus extra for dusting
55 g (2 oz/scant ½ cup) icing (confectioner's) sugar
1 medium free-range egg

FOR THE FILLING

225 g (8 oz/⅔ cup) golden syrup
225 ml (8 fl oz/scant 1 cup) double (heavy) cream
finely grated zest of 1 orange
finely grated zest of 1 lemon and juice of ½
2 Granny Smith apples, peeled, cored and grated
½ teaspoon Cornish sea salt
1 medium free-range egg, beaten
75 g (2½ oz/scant 1 cup) fresh white breadcrumbs

First, make the sweet pastry. Place the butter, flour and icing sugar in a food processor and blitz until it resembles breadcrumbs. Add the egg and pulse until the dough comes together and away from the sides. Transfer the dough to a floured work surface and shape into a round, then wrap in cling film (plastic wrap) and refrigerate for at least 2 hours. This can always be made a day ahead or make several batches and freeze, so you always have some pastry to hand.

Preheat the oven to 200°C (180°C fan/400°F/Gas 6). Line a 22 cm (9 in) fluted tart tin with a circle of greaseproof paper.

Remove the pastry from the refrigerator and roll it out to about 2mm (⅛ in) thick. Carefully line the tin with the pastry, then place back in the refrigerator to chill.

Line the chilled pastry case with some greaseproof paper and tumble in some ceramic baking beans, Bake blind for 15 minutes, then remove the baking beans and greaseproof and cook the pastry case for a further 2 minutes. Remove from the oven and set aside.

For the filling, gently heat the syrup, cream, orange and lemon zest, lemon juice, grated apple and salt together in a pan. Remove from the heat and whisk in the egg, then add the breadcrumbs and stir together.

Fill the tart case with the filling and cook for 20–25 minutes until set and golden brown. Allow to cool.

Slice with a hot knife – this will give nice clean edges to your slices. Serve with my No-Churn Clotted Cream Ice Cream (see page 214) or some clotted cream.

COOK'S NOTES Another method I love to use, which my grandmother always swore by, is to grate the pastry into the tin and then pat the pastry out with your hands to line the tin. Always handle pastry with care and do not overwork. If time is an issue, ready-bought pastry from supermarkets really is good. If you do not have ceramic baking beans, rice is a perfect replacement. Any leftover pastry can be used to make jam tarts.

No-Churn Clotted Cream Ice Cream with Grannie Jean's Chocolate Sauce

I love ice cream and I love it throughout the seasons. I also love my ice-cream maker and recommend investing in one. If you don't have one, however, my no-churn ice cream works a treat.

Grannie Jean was a capable person on every level. A paediatric doctor in her time, which was a remarkable achievement for a woman in the 1940s, Grannie was also a very good cook and gardener, and everything always had to be just right. I always had a bit of a passion for Bird's Ice Magic chocolate sauce (remember that), which always set hard as you poured it over the ice cream. From my child's point of view, this was the best thing ever, but Grannie actually made the dreamiest, glossiest, rich and perfectly sweet chocolate sauce, which she always served with her vanilla ice cream. I could have drunk it straight from the jug. It was a highlight of family barbecues.

SERVES 4–6

FOR THE ICE CREAM
1 x 400 g (14 oz) tin of sweetened condensed milk
1 x 600 g (1 lb 5 oz) pot of Roddas's clotted cream
1 vanilla pod, split

GRANNIE JEAN'S CHOCOLATE SAUCE:

FOR THE CHOCOLATE MIXTURE
125 g (4 oz) dark chocolate (70% cocoa solids), broken into small pieces
330 g (11 oz/scant 1½ cups) caster (superfine) sugar
375 ml (12 fl oz/1½ cups) water

FOR THE COCOA MIXTURE
300 ml (10 fl oz/1¼ cups) water
1½ tablespoons cornflour (cornstarch), slaked with a little of the water first
125 g (4 oz/1 cup) cocoa powder

TO FINISH
a knob of unsalted butter
a pinch of Cornish sea salt

For the ice cream, put the condensed milk and cream into a large mixing bowl and scrape in the seeds from the vanilla pod. Beat with an electric whisk until thick.

Pour the mixture into a 450 g (1 lb) loaf tin (pan), cover with cling film (plastic wrap) and freeze until frozen. I can never resist giving it a stir every 30 minutes for extra smoothness (see, no ice-cream maker required).

For the chocolate sauce, first make the chocolate mixture. Put the dark chocolate, sugar and water into a heavy-based pan over a low heat. Heat, stirring occasionally, until the chocolate has melted and the sugar has dissolved. Remove from the heat.

Next, make the cocoa mixture. In a bowl, mix the water, slaked cornflour and cocoa until well combined, then pour into the pan with the melted chocolate mixture. Place back on the heat and slowly bring to the boil, stirring until thickened.

To finish, add a knob of butter and a pinch of salt, and stir to a glossy sauce.

COOK'S NOTES Try adding the zest and sieved juice of 1 lemon and 2 tablespoons of runny honey for a delicious no-churn lemon and honey clotted cream ice cream. The chocolate sauce freezes well, too. Melted Mars bars with a dash of milk make the most delicious quick alternative.

To lift your spirits

A drinks cupboard, or tray, is perhaps one of those things that I think should be essential in the house. I am not suggesting you need to reach for a tipple all the time, but for me there are those cooking moments that will always call for Calvados in my tarte tatin, or Grand Marnier for my profiteroles, Noilly Prat for the *beurre blanc*, or simply some brandy to feed my Christmas cake. I promise, you will not look back – and, of course, it is very useful to have to hand whenever you do want to shake a cocktail at home.

Bloody Mary

Always spicy and essential for a hangover, my mouth waters at the thought of this tomatoey uplifting drink, which is basically vodka and cold tomato juice spiced up to your own taste. Fresh celery (always with the leaves) make a wonderful stirrer and I sometimes add a pinch of celery salt too.

MAKES 1

50 ml (1¾ fl oz/3 tablespoons) vodka (my citrus vodka in collaboration with Colwith Farm Distillery – see page 220 – works particularly well)
15 ml (½ fl oz/1 teaspoon) Pedro Ximénez sherry
150 ml (5 fl oz/scant ⅔ cup) good-quality tomato juice (very cold)
4 dashes of Worcestershire Sauce
Tabasco sauce dashes (1 = mild; 3 = medium; 6 = hot)
a pinch of Cornish sea salt
ice cubes

TO GARNISH
celery stick
lemon slice

Combine all the ingredients, except the garnish, in a mixing glass over ice and gently stir. Taste and consider as you make it. A little more lemon, pepper, more spice or ice – make this how you like to drink it.

Strain into a tall glass (for me, no ice) and garnish.

COOK'S NOTE Very cold tomato juice – do not compromise on this. I love a little sea salt on the end of the celery stirrer before eating it. If making more than one, leave the Tabasco out and let your friends spice up their own. Hangover, what hangover?

Cornish Wrecker

This beauty is fit for a queen. It is the cocktail we served at the G7 summit in the summer of 2021, at the Eden Project, to Her Majesty the Queen, the Royal Family and distinguished guests. Clotted cream gin, coconut rum, gorse-flower syrup and soda on the rocks. Cornwall in a glass. What an adventure.

MAKES 1

50 ml (1¾ fl oz/3 tablespoons) Wrecking Coast clotted cream gin (or your favourite gin)
12.5 ml (½ fl oz/2½ teaspoons) coconut rum
1½ tablespoons lemon juice
1½ tablespoons Gorse Flower Syrup (see below)
ice cubes

TO FINISH
soda water
1 lemon twist (or slice)
edible flowers (I use borage)

GORSE-FLOWER SYRUP
100 ml (3½ fl oz/scant ½ cup) water
200 g (7 oz/scant 1 cup) caster (superfine) sugar
2 handfuls of gorse flowers
2 drops of natural coconut flavouring

First, make the gorse-flower syrup. In a saucepan, heat the water, sugar, gorse flowers and coconut flavouring over a very low heat for about 30 minutes until the sugar has dissolved, the flowers have wilted and the syrup has changed to a gentle yellow colour. Remove from the heat and leave to infuse and cool for at least 6 hours, or overnight. Use as required.

To make the cocktail, shake all the ingredients, except the soda water and garnish, together in an ice-filled cocktail shaker until super cold.

Pour over ice and top up with soda water. Add a lemon twist and a borage flower to garnish.

COOK'S NOTE Any good-quality gin will work deliciously in this drink. Always have some ice in the freezer.

Dirty Vodka Martini

Classic and always hits the spot. A reminder (to myself only): just the one, otherwise I forget my name.

MAKES 1

50 ml (1¾ fl oz/ 3 tablespoons) Colwith Farm Emily Scott Citrus Vodka (see Cook's notes)
1 tablespoon chilled dry vermouth
1½ tablespoons olive brine
ice cubes
1 lemon wedge
1 green olive, to garnish

Pour the gin, vermouth and olive brine over a handful of ice in a cocktail shaker and shake.

Run a lemon wedge around the edge of a chilled martini glass and strain in the cocktail. Garnish with a whole green olive.

COOK'S NOTES

Chill the glass in the freezer so it is extra cold.

Gin or vodka – whatever you fancy.

Citrus fruits are wheels of sunshine that bring colour and deliciousness to my kitchen all year round – they are very much essential ingredients in my cooking. Perhaps this is why I chose to make a citrus vodka for my delicious collaboration with Colwith Farm Distillery. Soft, clean, with creamy vanilla undertones and bright, fragrant sherbet notes, it is a must for any drinks cabinet. Colwith Farm made a wonderful pairing as we have a shared ethos – everything they produce is made from scratch on their Cornwall estate, so provenance is key. The connection between the land and sea and the food and drink that finds its way to our tables is very close to my heart.

Time

to

(THERAPY)

Preserve

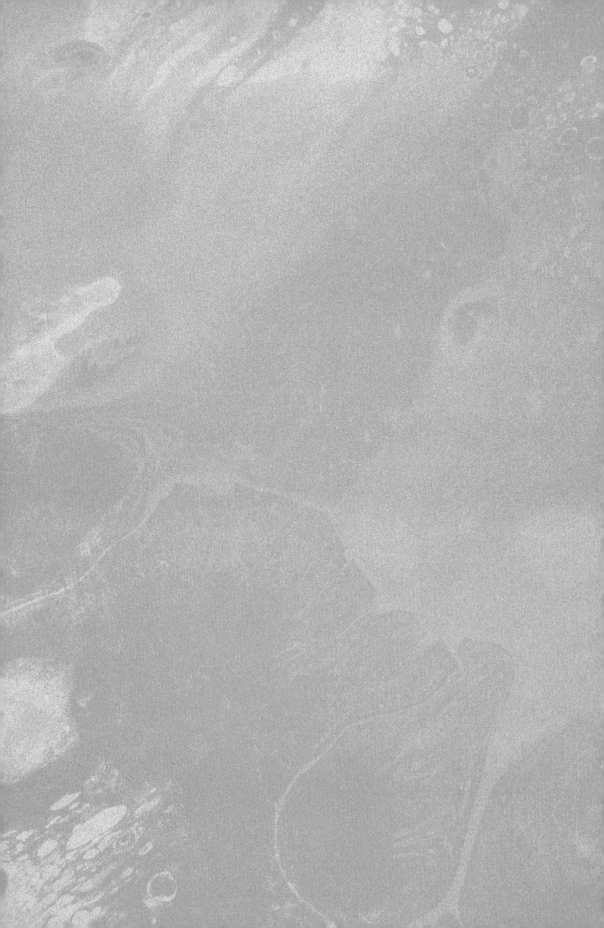

SPARE TIME means time to preserve the rich pickings of the garden and hedgerows, whatever the season. In our busy, fraught lives, it's worth making some space in your life for kitchen therapy – it truly is time well spent. A little organisation is all it takes: writing a list, dusting off the jars in the back of the cuppboard, and making jellies, jams and compôtes to be enjoyed for the rest of the year. Routines are important, they ground me, but rituals are nourishing – they feed you, your family and friends. For me, the process of preserving berries and making jams is life-enhancing.

Toast & jam, jam & toast

A note on toast and what it means to me. Toast is my go-to comfort food. It never disappoints and always gives me that needed hug. Sunday-night toast was always a thing when I was growing up and it still is – a mug of tea, butter and Marmite. Salty deliciousness. Then there is peanut butter, usually when suitably hungover. I save jam for breakfast, as a sweet lift to my day ahead, the fruits preserved when they are in season to enjoy all year round. (Butter always.)

Bramble, Apple & Bay Jam

The bramble season is relatively short and I always find myself picking more than I can eat, so freezing or preserving them is always high on my list in the autumn. Perhaps more a jelly than a jam, this is a wonderful way to use up hedgerow brambles and perfect for a cheese board or spread on toast.

MAKES 4 X 320 G (11 OZ) JARS

450 g (1 lb) blackberries
2 cooking apples, peeled, cored and chopped
150 ml (5 fl oz/scant ⅔ cup) water
450 g (1 lb/2 cups) jam (preserving) sugar
juice of 1 lemon
2 bay leaves

Pick through and wash the blackberries, then place them in a heavy-based saucepan along with the apples and measured water. Cook them very gently with a lid on for 20–25 minutes, then mash to a pulp (I find a potato masher is the best way to reduce them into a pulp).

Add the sugar, lemon juice and bay leaves to the pan and return to the heat, gently allowing the sugar to dissolve. This takes time, try not to be impatient and wait until every grain of sugar is dissolved. Remove the bay leaves and bring the mixture gently up to a rolling boil, then cook for a further 10 minutes, stirring constatnly to avoid the fruit sticking to the pan. It will foam up, so skim off the scum and keep the heat under control.

Line a fine mesh sieve with a muslin (cheesecloth) and set it over a large bowl. Pour in the jam mixture and use a wooden spoon to push all the fruit and juice through, bringing the muslin together at the end to squeeze out any remaining juice.

Pour into sterilised jars (see Cook's note), cover with discs of waxed paper, cool and then cover with lids. Once opened, it will keep for up to 6 months in the refrigerator or a cool pantry.

COOK'S NOTE To sterilise jars, wash the jars and lids in warm, soapy water, rinse well, then dry them thoroughly with a clean dish towel. Place them on a baking tray and pop in a 200°C (180°C fan/400°F/Gas 6) oven for 10 minutes. If you have a high temperature cycle on your dishwasher, this is an option, too.

Apricot & Lavender Compôte

A touch of golden sunshine in a jar for your breakfast bowl, toast or as a topping for summer berries.

MAKES 2 X 250 G (9 OZ) JARS

300 g (10½ oz) apricots
150 ml (5 fl oz/scant ⅔ cup) water
80 g (3 oz/⅓ cup) golden caster (superfine) sugar
1 vanilla pod (bean), split
2 teaspoons lavender flowers

Wash and cut the apricots in half and remove the stones (pits). Place in a heavy-based saucepan and add the measured water, then add the sugar, vanilla pod and lavender flowers. Slowly bring to a simmer, ensuring the sugar dissolves, and cook until the fruit has softened.

Spoon into a sterilised jar (see page 227) and store in the refrigerator for 2–3 days. It also freezes well in small batches.

COOK'S NOTE If you have a lot of lavender, which I usually do in the summer, make some lavender sugar by blitzing 1 kg (2 lb 4 oz/4⅓ cups) caster (superfine) sugar with 4 teaspoons of lavender flowers. Store in an airtight jar and use when needed. Swap out the rose petals in my shortbread recipe on page 66 for lavender sugar and flowers.

Strawberry & Elderflower Jam

Strawberries and elderflowers are a great match. Beautiful, creamy white elderflowers are so delicate and pretty and have a short season, so seize the moment to make your own cordial and this delightful jam, which is a wonderful way to preserve summer and tether down those warmer days, bringing sunshine to the greyer days of the year. Pick your own strawberries, if you have time.

MAKES 3 X 320 G (11 OZ) JARS

700 g (1 lb 9 oz/ generous 3 cups) jam (preserving) sugar
900 g (2 lb) in-season strawberries
50 ml (1¾ fl oz/3 tablespoons) elderflower cordial (for home-made, see Harlyn Elderflower Cordial in my previous book, *Sea & Shore*, or use store-bought)
juice of 1 lemon
20 g (¾ oz) unsalted butter (optional)

Preheat the oven to 190°C (170°C fan/340°F/Gas 3).

Spread the jam sugar over a baking tray and place in the oven for 15 minutes.

Meanwhile, wash, dry and hull the strawberries and layer them in a preserving pan.

Remove the hot sugar syrup from the oven and carefully pour it over the strawberries. Add the elderflower cordial and lemon juice, cover and leave for at least 12 hours or – even better – 24 hours, to macerate.

When ready to cook, bring the pan to the boil, then reduce to a simmer and cook for 30 minutes. After this time, bring it back to a rolling boil for 10 minutes or until the mixture reaches 110°C (230°F) on a sugar thermometer. Leave to cool slightly.

If there is scum sitting on the surface of the jam, stir in the teaspoon of butter, as this helps disperse it. Ladle into sterilised jars (see page 227), top with discs of waxed paper and seal while the jam is still warm. Label and date, and store in a cool, dark place for up to 1 year. Once opened, it will keep for up to 6 months in the refrigerator or a cool pantry.

COOK'S NOTE Dollop on top of rice pudding (see page 106) or serve with a traditional cream tea (jam first) with clotted cream.

Sugared Fruit Jellies

My grandmother Marnie would frequently make fruit jellies for us. Always a sticky glorious mess. They would be kept high up out of reach on the bookshelf in little paper cases, but it became a game and a highlight to try to reach for them and they would be given to us as treats. I always remember that sweet and sour taste on my tongue. I totally blame Marnie for the sweet tooth I have today. Recreating these transports me back to fond memories of time spent with my grandparents.

MAKES 20 JELLIES

- vegetable oil, for greasing
- 900 g (2 lb/scant 3 cups) jam of choice (blackcurrant is my favourite)
- juice of 2 lemons
- caster (superfine) sugar, for dusting

Grease a small square tray with vegetable oil.

Combine the jam and lemon juice in a saucepan and bring to a rolling boil, stirring until the mixture has reduced and resembles a sticky paste.

Pour the jam mixture into the prepared tray and leave to cool and set at room temperature for at least 12 hours or overnight.

Turn the set jelly out and use a hot knife to cut it into squares or roll it into balls. Dust with caster sugar. Store between layers of baking parchment in the refrigerator.

COOK'S NOTE Blackcurrants, redcurrants and blackberries all make a great jelly.

Quince & Pear Mincemeat

Slow-roasted quince, spices and the fruits of Christmas combine in a mincemeat for all those mince pies encased in short buttery pastry. This is a recipe from the archive of Grannie Jean – she would have loved seeing our family recipes coming to life in my books. One of her notes (Grannie wrote everything down) reads: 'Quince really are quite tricky, but worth it.' This recipe is rich with all the scents of Christmas and really worth making yourself.

MAKES ABOUT 4 X 370 G (13 OZ) JARS

2 baked quince (see below)
1 pear, peeled, cored and chopped
175 g (6 oz/scant 1½ cups) raisins
175 g (6 oz/scant 1½ cups) dried cranberries
175 g (6 oz/scant 1¼ cups) currants
175 g (6 oz/ scant 1½ cups) sultanas (golden raisins)
50 g (2 oz/generous ½ cup) flaked (slivered) almonds
75 g (2½ oz/scant ½ cup) chopped dried figs
125 g (4 oz) unsalted butter (or suet, if you prefer)
200 g (7 oz/generous 1 cup) soft dark brown sugar
2 teaspoons ground cinnamon
2 teaspoons mixed spice
1 teaspoon grated nutmeg
zest of 1 lemon
zest of 1 orange
200 ml (7 fl oz/scant 1 cup) brandy (or rum or sherry)

FOR THE BAKED QUINCE
2 quince
115 g (3¾ oz/½ cup) caster (superfine) sugar
zest of ½ lemon
1 fresh bay leaf
1 vanilla pod, split
60 ml (2 fl oz/¼ cup) water

First, bake the quince. Preheat the oven to 150°C (130°C fan/ 300°F/Gas 1).

Rinse and wipe the quince clean. Quarter them lengthways but do not remove the pith or core. Put the quarters, cut-sides up, in a small baking tray (pan), sprinkle over the sugar and lemon zest and add the bay leaf and vanilla. Pour in the water, cover lightly with kitchen foil and bake in the oven for 2 hours, turning the fruit a couple of times. When the quince are soft, sticky and a beautiful burnt orange colour, they are ready.

Remove from the oven and allow to cool, then chop finely.

Put all the ingredients, except the brandy, into a large pan over a medium heat and stir together, allowing the butter to melt. Gently simmer for 10–15 minutes, then remove from the heat and pour in the brandy.

Ladle into sterilised jars (see page 227), top with discs of waxed paper and seal the jars while the mincemeat is still warm. Label and date, and store in a cool, dark place for up to 1 year. Once opened, it will keep for up to 6 months in the refrigerator or a cool pantry.

COOK'S NOTE This can be made up to 3 months in advance. Baking the quince gives the mincemeat a really fudgy texture and golden colour.

Hellyar's Seville Orange & Grapefruit Marmalade with Thyme

This is a ritual that my partner Mark and I do together with great happiness every January. A process of peeling, chopping, zesting, squeezing and, always, laughter. The result is golden jam jars full of delicious marmalade that will see us through the year. Thyme leaves add a lovely herbal note. I sometimes use rosemary, too.

MAKES 8 X 320 G (11 OZ) JARS

- 1 kg (2 lb 4 oz) Seville oranges
- 2 large grapefruit
- 2 lemons
- 2.5 litres (87 fl oz/ 10 cups) water
- 2 kg (4 lb 8 oz/8⅔ cups) jam (preserving) sugar
- 1 small bunch of thyme, leaves only
- 1 teaspoon unsalted butter (optional)

Place the fruit whole into a large preserving pan and pour in the water. Slowly bring to the boil and simmer for 2 hours. Allow to cool. Use a slotted spoon to remove the fruit to a colander set over a bowl (reserve the liquid in the pan) and allow it to drain.

Line a large bowl with muslin (cheesecloth). Halve the fruit and scoop out all of the pulp, pips, pith – or gubbins, as we call it – and place it all in the cloth. Tie the cloth into a tight bag, then squeeze out as much liquid as possible into the pan of reserved liquid. All these juices contain pectin, which are essential for setting the marmalade. Use kitchen string to tie the bag onto the side of the preserving pan so that it is suspended in the water.

With a sharp knife, slice the remaining fruit peels into quarters, then shred to your preferred thickness. I love this process – it feels therapeutic, as if time stops briefly and I can get lost in just making marmalade.

Attach a sugar thermometer to the side of the pan (or have it ready if it is the hand-held type). Add the shredded peel and jam sugar to the pan along with the thyme leaves and stir in with a whisk. Bring up to a rolling boil and cook for 15–20 minutes, stirring occasionally. When the marmalade reaches 105°C (221°F) on the thermometer (or see Cook's note for wrinkle test), remove from the heat and allow to cool slightly.

If there is scum on the surface of the marmalade, stir in the teaspoon of butter, as this helps disperse it. Ladle into sterilised jars (see page 227), top with discs of waxed paper and seal while still warm. Label and date, and store in a cool, dark place. Once opened, it will keep for up to 6 months in the refrigerator or a cool pantry. Dollop on to porridge, spread on your toast, make bread-and-butter pudding or marmalade almond tarts.

COOK'S NOTE A jam thermometer, ladle and funnel are great tools in which to invest if you are preserving fruits. If you don't have a thermometer, use the wrinkle test. Chill a saucer in your freezer. After 15–20 minutes at a rolling boil, spoon a teaspoon of marmalade onto the chilled plate and leave it for 1 minute. If the marmalade wrinkles when pushed gently, it is ready; if not, return to the boil for 5–10 minutes, then repeat the wrinkle test.

Preserved Summer Tomatoes in Good Olive Oil

On toast with basil oil, summer tomatoes are simply the best. This is a lovely way of preserving them to allow you to enjoy them in recipes in the colder months.

MAKES 1 X 1.5 L (50 FL OZ) JAR

- 500 g (1 lb 2 oz) cherry tomatoes
- 3 teaspoons caster (superfine) sugar
- 1 teaspoon chilli (hot pepper) flakes
- a pinch of Cornish sea salt
- 4 black peppercorns
- 1 bunch of thyme
- 6 garlic cloves, peeled
- 300 ml (10 fl oz/1¼ cups) good olive oil

Preheat the oven to 140°C (120°C fan/275°F/Gas ½).

Cut all the tomatoes in half and place them in a roasting pan. Sprinkle over the sugar, chilli flakes and salt, add the peppercorns, tuck the thyme sprigs and garlic cloves in among the tomatoes and pour over the olive oil.

Roast in the oven for 2½ hours.

Spoon into sterilised jars (see page 227). They will keep for up to a year stored in a cool larder or pantry. Once opened, they will keep for up to a week in the refrigerator.

COOK'S NOTE Another way to preserve tomatoes is to slowly roast them without olive oil to dry them out so they become chewy, sweet and delicious, similar to a sunblush tomato, but your own.

Damson & Plum Jam

Gathered from our tree, damsons are wild and beautiful, and oh the colour ... They are so rewarding to cook with and easy to love. Try them in compôtes, crumbles, ice cream and jam for your toast. I always serve this jam with my butterflied leg of lamb on a Sunday (see page 194).

MAKES 8 X 320 G (11 OZ) JARS

1 kg (2 lb 4 oz) damsons
600 ml (20 fl oz/ 2½ cups) water
2 kg (4 lb 8 oz) plums, halved and stoned (pitted)
1 kg (2 lb 4 oz/4⅓ cups) jam (preserving) sugar
a knob of unsalted butter
juice of 1 lemon

Wash the damsons in a colander and remove their stalks and any leaves. Place the damsons and water in a preserving pan and bring to the boil, then reduce to a simmer and cook until soft. Let cool slightly, then drain the damsons in a fine mesh sieve over a large bowl to catch all the juices and push through as much juice as possible (disposable gloves are a good idea here). Discard the pits and skins.

Pour the liquid back into the preserving pan and attach a sugar thermometer to the pan. Add the plums and sugar, and slowly bring back to the boil, ensuring the sugar is dissolved. Rapidly boil until it reaches a setting point of 105°C (221°F). Stir the jam thoroughly, then stir in the knob of butter and the lemon juice. Remove any scum on the surface and simmer the jam for a further 5 minutes.

Remove from the heat, allow to cool slightly, then ladle into sterilised jars (see page 227), top with waxed paper seals and lids. Label and date, and store in a cool, dark place for up to 1 year. Once opened, it will keep for up to 6 months in the refrigerator or a cool pantry.

COOK'S NOTE Damsons are pretty versatile and can also be made into vodka, jellies, crumbles and cheese.

Caramel-Caped Gooseberries

Cape gooseberries dipped in caramel – I call these 'superheroes'. Beautiful, small and round, wrapped in a papery case, cape gooseberries, also know as physalis, are deliciously tart and sweet. A cross between a tomato and gooseberry in terms of flavour, they are lovely served at the end of a meal.

SERVES 4

200 g (7 oz/scant 1 cup) golden caster (superfine) sugar
4 tablespoons water
20 cape gooseberries (physalis)

Place the sugar and water in a small saucepan and set over a medium heat. Let the sugar dissolve and cook, without stirring, to a light brown caramel. Remove from the heat and immerse the bottom of the pan in cold water (this stops the caramel from cooking further).

Take the gooseberries by the leaves and individually dip the berries into the caramel. Place them on a sheet of baking parchment to set.

COOK'S NOTES Take great care when cooking caramel, as you can easily burn yourself. To remove any caramel stuck to the pan, bring the pan of water to the boil and allow to cool, then wash with hot soapy water. These are equally good dipped in melted chocolate.

Fruity, Boozy Christmas Cake (merry & bright)

SERVES 10

CAKE EVE
175 g (6 oz/scant 1½ cups) raisins
175 g (6 oz/scant 1½ cups) sultanas (golden raisins)
450 g (1 lb/3 cups) currants
100 g (3½ oz/½ cup) glacé cherries, halved
50 g (2 oz/¼ cup) dried cranberries
150 ml (5 fl oz/scant ⅔ cup) brandy (or sherry or rum), plus extra to 'feed' the cake

CAKE DAY
225 g (8 oz) unsalted butter, at room temperature
200 g (7 oz/generous 1 cup) dark brown sugar
zest of 1 lemon
zest of 1 orange
4 medium free-range eggs, at room temperature
2 tablespoons treacle or golden syrup
225 g (8 oz/generous 1¾ cups) plain (all-purpose) flour
½ teaspoon ground ginger
1 teaspoon ground cinnamon
1 teaspoon grated nutmeg
50 g (2 oz/½ cup) ground almonds

FROSTING (OPTIONAL*)
250 g (9 oz/1 cup) mascarpone or cream cheese
175 g (6 oz) unsalted butter, softened
200 g (7 oz/generous 1½ cups) icing (confectioners') sugar

(*OPTIONAL TOPPING, IF NOT FROSTING)
100 g (3½ oz/⅔ cup) blanched almonds
3 tablespoons apricot jam, warmed, for brushing

Kitchenside at home and happy in my work. Mid-November and it is Cake Eve (as we call it – it's more commonly known as Stir-Up Sunday), a time I really love – the festive glow, the table, a sense of place, plotting and planning my menu, sharing food and wine, laughter, merriment and conversation, all the comfort and joy. There is an order to things – *mise en place* – that makes me so content. The fruit soaking happily in brandy can be left overnight or longer if you want. I prepare the other ingredients ready for action the next day. Worth getting ahead.

I think I may be turning into my grandmother (good or bad), as I am finding contentment in rituals rather than routines. There is something so comforting in being able to reach for a slice of cake that you have lovingly made, whether you are baking a fruit cake just because or as part of your Christmas celebrations.

CAKE EVE
Place all the dried fruit in a saucepan with the booze and bring to a simmer, then pour into a bowl and leave to cool. Cover and leave to soften overnight.

CAKE DAY
Preheat the oven to 160°C (140°C fan/320°F/Gas 2). Line the base and sides of a 20 cm (8 in) round cake tin (pan) with a double layer of greaseproof paper. You will need the side lining to be a good 8 cm (3 in) higher than the tin.

If you would like your cake to be particularly moist, blitz half the soaked fruit in a food processor to make a paste, and stir it back into the rest of the fruit (worth it).

In a large bowl, cream the butter and sugar until light and fluffy. Grate in the lemon and orange zest and beat in the eggs, one at a time. Mix in the treacle or golden syrup.

In a separate bowl, sift the flour with the spices and ground almonds. Mix into the batter in parts, alternating with the soaked fruit. Spoon the batter into the lined tin.

Bake in the oven for about 4 hours. Check after 2½ hours and then every 20 minutes – it is ready when an inserted skewer comes out clean.

As soon as the cake comes out of the oven, brush with a little more brandy (essential). Leave to cool in the tin for 10 minutes, then remove, placing it onto a large sheet of kitchen foil.

Wrap it up twice to retain the heat for as long as possible. After a few hours, remove the foil and wrap the cake up again in a double sheet of greaseproof paper and a double sheet of foil. Make sure you can get to the top of the cake to feed it. Store in an airtight container for up to 12 weeks. During this time, feed the cake once a week with the alcohol of your choice by gently pouring 1–2 tablespoonfuls over the top and rewrapping.

FROSTING
This cake is a no marzipan affair for me. I love icing my cake with a soft topping (similar to my carrot cake topping in *Sea & Shore*) made by whipping together the mascarpone or cream cheese and softened butter with the icing sugar. Evenly spread the frosting over the cake and decorate with festive leaves.

*If you prefer no frosting, I like to decorate the top of the cake with blanched whole almonds arranged in a circular pattern on top of the batter just before baking. I then glaze the top with some warm apricot jam to finish.

COOK'S NOTE Before starting, and to get most enjoyment out of making your very own fruit cake, get organised with all your ingredients and tools, and line your cake tin at the beginning. Of course, this cake can be made at any time of the year, it's not just for Christmas.

Index

Acknowledgements: All the Love

Time is everything, but sometimes time stops. There are moments in time when you need to stand still and reflect on what has been created. I feel very lucky to have been given the opportunity to write this book – book two, what a dream. Some days it felt hard to find the words lost in my mind. I would hide from my to-do list and procrastinate. Finally, here it is and my heart is full. It is a beautiful, collective thing writing a book, from my vision and words to the dream team of publisher, food stylists, prop stylist, photographer and so many more – so many people to thank and appreciate.

My children, Oscar, Finn and Evie, for you always.

Mark, for your patience and ability not to react, your support throughout this project and beyond has been so important to me. Ditto.

To Phillippe, for your friendship and generosity.

To Liane, you have taught me so much about myself. Here is to self love.

Kajal, my publisher and friend, thank you for everything, for believing in me and this book.

Emily, Chelsea, Emma and all at Hardie Grant, thank you for navigating me through this process with such professionalism, warmth and fun.

Thank you Kristin, you are a beautiful person and your talent for seeing detail, space and elegance is immeasurable. Days spent with you are magical.

Tabitha, simply a dreamy time with you, how you just bring together what is totally right, every time. Our chats and putting the world to rights (snogs).

Tamara, your energy, your ability to multitask and you just know how I think and feel about cooking. What a joy to work with you on this book.

Charlotte, you are wonderful, thank you so much.

Annie, my recipe tester, thank you for your wise words always and passion for cooking. Until next time.

Sabhbh, my agent, you are simply the best person. I love your gentle directness, style and calm ways, your love for books, and your love and support for this book.

Thank you to Felicity and all at Curtis Brown. I love being represented by you.

To my team at Emily Scott Food, you know who you are. Thank you for being on this adventure with me.

Fill your glass with hope and simple pleasures, embrace opportunities and say yes.

Emily x